*Your life
is your canvas.*

*What will you
paint?*

# The *Art* of Living Alone

## A Practical Guidebook for Blissful Solo Domesticity

Jennifer Lynn O'Hara

Copyright © 2018 Jennifer Lynn O'Hara

All rights reserved.

ISBN-10: 0-9993738-1-1
ISBN-13: 978-0-9993738-1-1

This book is dedicated to everyone who has dared to live the unexpected life.

# ACKNOWLEDGMENTS

Big thanks go to....

Dave, for dedicating your life to keeping others safe.
Malinda, for your invaluable input.
Christina & Sam, for being so amazing.
Steve, for everything you do.
All my friends who shared their advice and insight.

# CONTENTS

| | | |
|---|---|---|
| 1 | A Little Background | 1 |
| 2 | The Unexpected Life | 7 |
| 3 | Safety | 15 |
| 4 | Furnishings | 31 |
| 5 | Grocery Shopping | 43 |
| 6 | Cooking | 53 |
| 7 | Dining Out | 65 |
| 8 | Sleeping | 75 |
| 9 | Social Life | 83 |
| 10 | Fitness | 93 |
| 11 | Emotional/Mental Health | 103 |
| 12 | Finances | 117 |
| 13 | Surviving the Holidays | 127 |
| 14 | Sometimes It's No Fun | 141 |
| 15 | Staying Motivated | 147 |
| 16 | One Last Thing | 155 |
| | References | 159 |

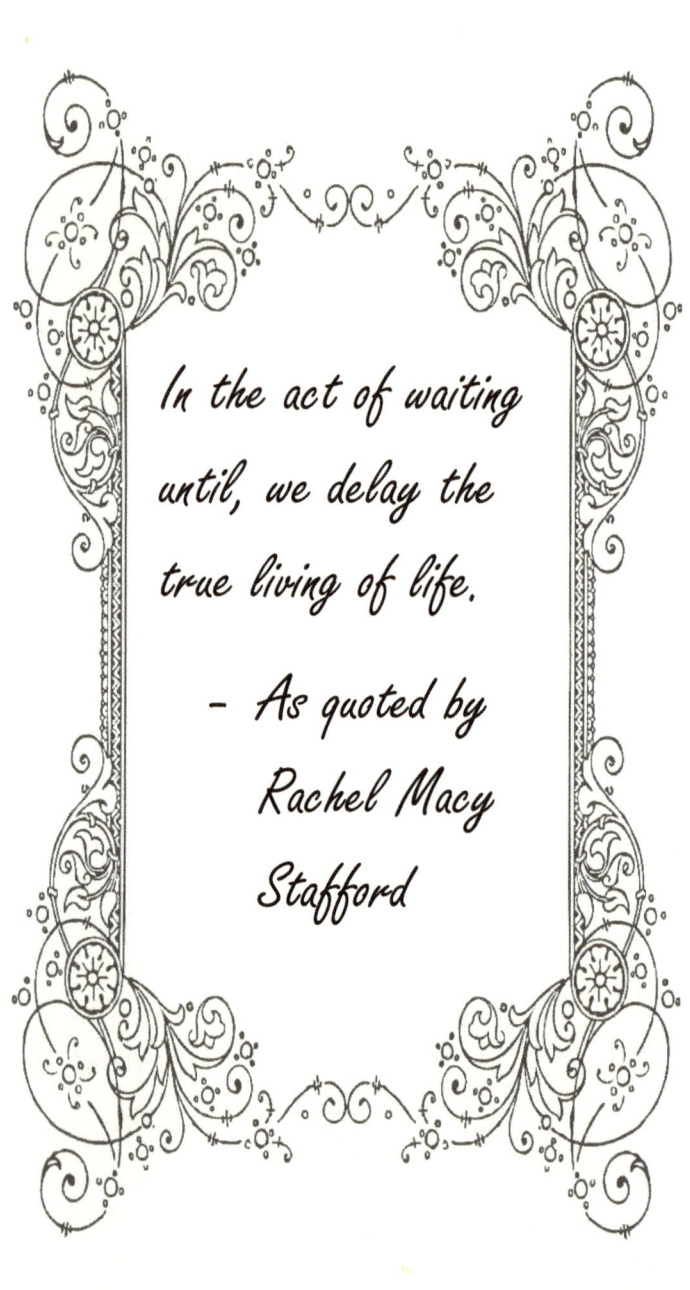

In the act of waiting until, we delay the true living of life.

— As quoted by Rachel Macy Stafford

# A LITTLE BACKGROUND

A book about living alone. Why? I mean, aren't single people just sad spinsters and bachelors who are desperately looking for someone to marry so they don't have to live alone anymore? Why do we need a book about living alone when no one really wants to do so?

Well, let me tell you... Because none of that is actually true.

Sure, many singletons do want to get married. But

the trends for solo domesticity have changed dramatically in the last few decades, and forecasts point to a continuation, and acceleration, of those trends in years to come.

Census data in the U.S. and Canada show that the percentage of single person households is on the rise. In fact, global statistics indicate that the number of people choosing to remain single and live alone is the highest it's been since the 1800s, and that rate seems to be continuing its upward trend. Recent studies show that in developed countries as much as 50% or more of people of marriageable age are single. And many of those people are *choosing* to live alone.

Data around the health aspects of living alone is evolving, too. In decades past, researchers found that married people were healthier, happier, and lived longer than never-marrieds. But times, they are a-changing! A sociologist from Rutgers University has found that the health/happiness/longevity gap between marrieds and non-marrieds has narrowed to almost nothing. As more and more people delay getting married, or choose to never marry at all, staying single and living alone has become more acceptable in today's society. And the stress and social isolation around the single status has ebbed. But that doesn't mean it's any easier.

Despite these trends, society still seems obsessed with

couples, families, and relationships. Most of the singles' "how-to" guides are not focused on how to live alone successfully and contentedly; they are focused on how to find a mate or how to date or how to pick up someone or how to attract someone. Those topics are valid and important – many of us would love to find a person we can share our lives with. But what do we do until then? Do we have to put our lives on hold until Prince/Princess Charming shows up? On the contrary, this is the perfect time to live life to its fullest, to experience all those things that would be difficult to do once tied down to a spouse and kids, to enjoy the freedom and empowerment that living alone provides. But how do we do all that while also overcoming the challenges that come with solo domesticity? That's what this book is all about.

In the pages that follow, I will not attempt to explain the historic need for relationships and communal groups, nor will I try to pinpoint the cause of the modern phenomenon of solo living we are currently experiencing. There is a wealth of information on those topics that is easily accessible if you want to learn more. Instead, I humbly offer a summary of my life experiences – what I've learned after decades of my own solo domesticity – in hopes that it may help you find your own solo bliss.

I call this book *The Art of Living Alone* because solo

domesticity is an art form. And just like an art form, if it's worth doing, it's worth doing well and to the best of your ability. It should not be treated as a form of purgatory, a transitional period to be endured, or a waiting period for something better to come along. Instead, it should be celebrated, enjoyed, and reveled in as the glorious time of ultimate freedom and empowerment that it is.

I want to make the caveat that this book is not about marriage-bashing, or man-bashing, or woman-bashing, or relationship-bashing. It is merely a reflection of the times we're in (at the time of publication, that is). Despite the rising numbers of singles, society is still geared toward the expectation of marriage – especially if you're a woman. Consequently, there is less helpful advice for singles than there is for couples.

While this book will most likely be bought and read by women, it is applicable to men as well. In fact, some might argue that men might need it *more* than women. A sociologist from the University of Chicago has found that men living alone tend to fare worse than women living alone because men generally have a smaller social network to provide support. They also have a greater propensity for developing bad health habits without a partner to encourage them otherwise.

This book is intended to be a guidebook of helpful hints, tips, tricks, and advice for both men and women to live their best, most rewarding lives, not in spite of their single status, but *because* of it. Many of the chapters overlap a bit. This is on purpose. Most areas of our lives impact other areas of our lives – it is a natural domino effect. This book is designed to address the most significant parts of our lives that are affected by living alone, and offer suggestions and guidance of how to turn those challenges into advantages. (Or at the very least, minimize their negative impact.)

And bonus: Creating joy and happiness in your life now, and living your best and fullest life as a singleton, will ultimately make you a much more interesting person when your Prince or Princess Charming does decide to show up.

Your single life is your art form, so what will you create?

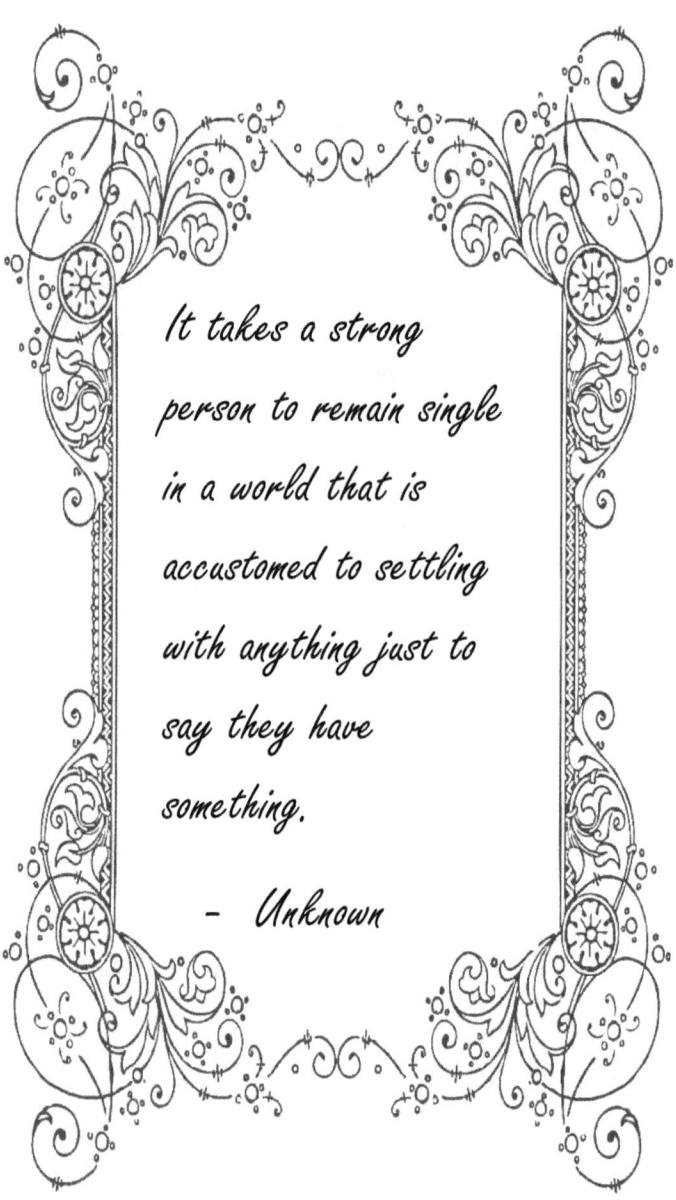

*It takes a strong person to remain single in a world that is accustomed to settling with anything just to say they have something.*

*— Unknown*

# THE UNEXPECTED LIFE

I was chatting with a friend a while ago, and she used a phrase that changed my life forever. She said, "Shoulds are dangerous."

*Shoulds are dangerous.*

In the days that followed, that phrase rolled over in my head and I began to understand the full implication of its meaning.

**Shoulds are dangerous.**

My life, and probably most of yours, has been affected by the word "should" in more ways than we ever realized.

From the cradle, our lives are shaped by shoulds.

- ✓ Girls should wear pink.
- ✓ Boys should wear blue.
- ✓ Girls should play with dolls.
- ✓ Boys should play with trucks.
- ✓ Girls should be kind and giving.
- ✓ Boys should be aggressive and powerful.

And the shoulds don't stop as we grow older.

- ✓ Women should be married by a certain age.
- ✓ Men should be the primary breadwinner.
- ✓ Women should have children.
- ✓ Men should have a career.
- ✓ Women should wait to buy a house until they're married.
- ✓ Men should be the ones to make the big decisions.

Society puts a lot of shoulds on our shoulders. Then, we top it off with our own personalized shoulds.

- ✓ I should be thinner.
- ✓ I should have more money.
- ✓ I should work out as much as my gym rat

friend.
- ✓ I should be as pretty as the women on TV.
- ✓ I should be happier.

Should, should, should….

All these shoulds leave us feeling unhappy, inadequate, and inferior. They keep us trapped in the pursuit of an unrealistic reality, and create a fear of social ostracization if we deviate too far from them.

The power of words is epic. In the Bible, the book of Proverbs is full of verses proclaiming that words can lift up or destroy, give life or kill. That's some serious power! If words have the ability to destroy or kill, how much more can they shape our lives – even without our conscious knowledge? The repercussions of shoulds are staggering.

So what happens when we dare to live the unexpected life?

As a single girl, I am forced to deal with the shoulds of my singlehood every day. Whether it is looks of shock or pity, prying questions, or disbelief and astonishment over my single status, the messages are clear: I "should" be married by now, I "should" want to have children, I "should" be looking for a husband, I "should" wait to do XYZ until I'm married. All that unwarranted judgment has only one result: to make me feel like there is something wrong with my life.

Here's a newsflash: There is nothing, ***nothing*** wrong with my life.

Is it worse to remain single, or to marry the wrong person because you feel society's pressure to marry? Is it worse to settle for a desk job with a steady paycheck, or risk it all to be an entrepreneur? Is it worse to passively fill the role society says you should, or to make waves by daring to define your own role and follow your dreams? It takes more courage and determination to live the unexpected life than to passively succumb to society's expectations.

Now, I'm not saying that people who choose to live a traditional life, who truly want those things, are wrong. For many people, the idea of a spouse and children and weeknight casseroles and a house in the burbs is what makes their hearts and souls sing. And for those people, I am happy. I am truly happy that what fulfills them also satisfies society's expectations. And there is nothing, ***nothing*** wrong with that life either.

But for the rest of us, living the unexpected life can have unexpected consequences.

In addition to fighting a never-ending battle to explain, defend, and justify our non-traditional choices, we must also battle the internal demons that tell us we're "not enough" because we have chosen to live differently than the crowd. As if that was not difficult enough, singles have added layers of challenges. We must figure out how to survive financially on just one income. If we falter or fall, there is no one there to pick us up. If we get tired, we have no one to lean on.

The challenge seems daunting. But the upsides of taking the risk can be very rewarding. To be brave enough to live the life we want to live, despite society's expectations, can yield unimaginable blessings. Life doesn't always work out the way we want or expect. But in the end, the knowledge that we gave it our best shot – that we took the risk, shrugged off the shoulds, and dared to live the unexpected life – leaves us with little to regret.

In recent years, trends have been changing. According to a recent study using data going back to 1880, marriage rates are at their lowest in nearly 150 years, and although divorce rates have seen a slight decline in recent decades, the overall trend of divorce rates are up. Additionally, according to the most recent U.S. Census, there are more single people in the U.S. than ever before (53% women, 47% men). Yet despite these statistics, society's expectations remain the same.

Henry David Thoreau said, "Most men lead lives of quiet desperation and go to the grave with the song still in them." How many songs have been silenced by shoulds? How much potential is untapped by the restraining power of words? When we bow to society's expectations, we end up doing, and missing, things we'll regret later. How sad to reach your last days and realize you haven't fully lived, only because the "should" overpowered your desire to create your own life.

So here and now I vow to shake the shoulds out of my life. I will throw off the bonds of society's expectations and live my life my way. Who's with me? Let's rattle society's cage and dare to be different.

Different is the new normal. *Vive la Différence!*

*Those who fly solo have the strongest wings.*

*– Anonymous*

# SAFETY

There are so many wonderful things about living alone. You can decorate your space any way you want. You don't have to put up with dirty socks or underwear on the floor. (Unless that's your thing, and then by all means, go nuts.) You can watch whatever chick-flick you want without suffering the eye rolls of a significant other. Sole-ownership of the remote control…ahhh…bliss.

But for me, none of that matters if I don't feel safe.

In order for me to relax and enjoy anything, I must know I'm safe – both physically and emotionally. Emotional safety is a subject we'll save for another chapter (or my therapist). For the purposes of this chapter, we'll focus on physical safety. After years of living alone, I have developed an arsenal of safety habits that I employ, no matter where I call home.

While writing this book, I conferred with my friend Dave Mather, who has 28 years' experience in law enforcement, both in uniform as a police lieutenant and now as an international law enforcement leadership consultant. Here are my top 10 tips, combined with Dave's advice, for safely living alone.

▶ **Leave your porch light on from dusk 'til dawn.** Would-be intruders prefer to work in secret, so if your home is lit up like the Vegas strip, an intruder is less likely to want to perform in a spotlight. Of course, if you're the type to forget to turn it on (like me), you can keep it on all the time. I use an LED bulb so it doesn't cost me a fortune to keep it lit. And if you have a back door be sure that is well lit too. I will often keep one downstairs light on all the time, too, even while I sleep. An intruder doesn't need to know if I'm actually awake or not.

**Dave's Tip:** Alternatively (and more energy efficient) would be to put a simple motion sensor on the light so that it turns on when people enter the sensor's field of view. There are a variety of installation options that range from simply screwing it into a light socket, to hard-wired options that require an electrician.

- **Put your lights on a timer.** During winter months it is often dark outside before my day's work is done. It's very scary, and potentially dangerous, to come home to a dark house. Having a programmable timer solves that problem. A programmable timer can turn the lights on for you at a set time when you're not at home. No more coming home to a dark house! These are also great for vacations. If I'm going to be gone for more than a day, I put my lights and TV on a timer. Having lights, and even sounds, coming on and off at various times every day gives the appearance that the home is inhabited, and not sitting empty just waiting to be robbed. I like the 3-prong kind that can handle several on/off times per day, can be programmed for a different schedule each day, and can accommodate two appliances or several lights. Randomness is key in creating a realistic illusion.

**Dave's Tip:** There are already some great options on the market (although fairly new ones) that use geo-fencing techniques on your smartphone to know when you're getting close to home and to turn the thermostat up (or down in summer) and the lights on. Also, to echo the recommendation of the randomness of a timer – the more random the times and locations are, the more it looks like someone is home.

- **Get a dog.** There are so many benefits of having a pet. One big benefit of dog ownership is that dogs reduce your risk of burglary. Large dogs, of course, are intimidating. But small dogs are also effective. Their warning barks are often enough to scare off someone with villainous intentions. Now, here is where I need to make an obvious warning statement. DO NOT get a dog just as a home security device. Dogs should be part of your family. And if you do not plan on treating them as such, and giving them the love and attention they require, (and frankly deserve), bypass this step and go on to #4.

**Dave's Tip:** Jack MacLean (*Secrets of a Superthief*) surveyed 300+ convicted and imprisoned property criminals and asked three questions:

> *Q. Would a dog scare you away?*
> A: 65% said a dog of good size and unpleasant disposition would.
>
> *Q: What kinds of dogs scare you?*
> A: 35% Dobermans, 30% Pit Bull breeds, 10% German Shepherds, 25% any dog.) In the follow up interviews, he believes that

more like 95% (instead of 65%) would be afraid of a big dog that sounds scary.

*Q: What would scare you away more than anything?*
A: 59% people in the house, 32% almost any dog, 9% [the night burglars] deterred by spot lights that light up the areas of ingress/egress.)

- **Invest in signage.** Believe it or not, most criminals can read. So having signage in front of your home can be an effective deterrent. It doesn't matter if the signs are true or not. A would-be intruder isn't going to stop and do a detailed analysis of whether your signs might be a ruse. They'll likely move on to the next unlit, dog-free house without signage. Signs can be "Beware of Dog," or "Smile, you're on camera!" or even a "Home Security" sign. The signs themselves are a deterrent, but don't go overboard and get all three. That will start to look fishy. Get one, or two at tops. Realism and believability are important here.

**Dave's Tip:** Signs have become so ubiquitous the common ones may be ignored. The same concept with a new and humorous twist may be more effective. Here are some examples:

Beware of dog = Our Great Dane welcomes

you as his meal.

We (picture of dog) can make it to the fence in three seconds – can you?

We might not be home but our dog is.

Attention Thieves: Please carry ID so we can notify next of kin.

- **You might have a house alarm, even if you don't.** Most cars today have remote keyless entries, and those remote keyless entries often come with a car alarm. Granted, most of the time they are "nuisance alarms" because they activate when we accidentally sit on the key fob or hit the wrong button. But in the case of someone trying to break into your home, they may be helpful. If your car is parked close enough to be activated by your remote, activating the alarm will cause unwanted attention which might be enough to scare away a bad guy.

**Dave's Tip:** There are some new home security systems that connect to your Wi-Fi and send notifications to your smartphone that include live video and pictures. Those systems are in the $200-$400 range and there are many great stories about people using the pictures to assist law enforcement with catching the people responsible. They may not prevent the actual break in, but may help ID and catch the criminal (which does have the advantage of making the neighborhood a bit safer).

- **Know the location of your closest police station.** I try to be constantly aware of my surroundings, even when driving. If I feel like I'm being followed home, the last thing I want to do is lead the stalker to my front door. Instead, I'll play follow-the-leader straight to the police station. Most of the time, the follower will turn off well before I reach the station. But on the off chance that the follower was a true stalker with ill-intent, the extra few minutes' detour would have been worthwhile. And, while we're on the subject of going home, sometimes the most dangerous walk for a single person can be the walk from the car to the front door. So take steps to look like a formidable opponent, a non-victim. Have your house key out and ready to go so you're not fumbling at the front door. Don't be distracted by texting or juggling packages. Walk tall, quickly, and confidently. Predators prey on the weak, so do your best to not look like prey.

**Dave's Tip:** Not all police stations are accessible 24 hours a day. It's important to know whether your local station is open. If you are really concerned, call 911 and let the dispatcher direct you where they need you to be. Most cellular phones (even ones without a plan) will connect with any open network for 911 calls. So even if you no longer can afford cell service, the phone should be able to dial 911 and get you connected.

- **Create the illusion that you don't live alone.** I am lucky enough to have two vehicles, one of which is a truck. I purposely did not girlify my truck because I want people to think a man drives it. I love having two cars, because even when I'm not home, one of my vehicles is, so it always looks like someone's home. And, when both vehicles are home, it looks like a man lives there. But if you don't have the luxury of having two vehicles, there are other ways to create the illusion. If you are a woman, buy a pair of extra-large men's boots from a local thrift store (the dirtier the better) and place them outside your front door, as if your big, burly husband/boyfriend/roommate took them off before entering his home. Be sure to move them occasionally, so they look freshly placed.

- **Get to know your neighbors even before you move in.** Before signing on the dotted line of a new home or apartment, check Megan's Law, and other crime websites to see who's living around you. Realtors can't say a lot about neighborhood demographics and crime stats, but every police officer I've talked to is more than happy to share how high/low incidents of crime are in my area. I usually ask them something like this, "If your daughter were considering moving into this neighborhood, what would you advise her?" The answers are very telling when you make it personal.

**Dave's Tip:** I second the recommendation of talking with the local officers. In addition, many agencies use online crime reporting software that helps you see what is going on in your neighborhood. Check websites like: crimereports.com, mylocalcrime.com, or crimemapping.com. The best way is to ask the local agency if their online data is available.

▸ **Make sure doors and windows are locked and secure.** When you move into a new home, the first thing you should do is change the locks. I'll never forget the terrifying night in my new home when some drunken friends of the previous owners decided to pay a visit. Of course I refused to open the door, but if they had a spare key, I may have been in serious trouble. If you live in an apartment, the apartment manager should be able to have the locks changed, or re-keyed. If you own your own home, make sure your doors are secured with deadbolt locks. Also, make sure windows have working locks. I go one step further and place dowels in the tracks of my windows and sliding doors. Of course, an intruder who really wants to get in could just break the glass. But breaking glass makes a very distinctive sound, and most intruders don't want to attract that kind of attention.

**Dave's Tip:** A good deadbolt is important in securing the main doors. Main doors should be solid wood or metal (not hollow). Additional locking security screen doors add extra layers someone has to get through (and additional time for someone to respond) if someone is trying to get in.

This is also a good place to talk about CPTED (Crime Prevention Through Environmental Design). The tenets of CPTED are too lengthy to discuss in-depth here, but a quick Google search will yield a wealth of information. Here's the quick take: 1) Improve outdoor lighting so you can see and be seen. 2) Create layers of access control, such as fences and thorny shrubs. But make sure none of those things create places for lurkers to hide. 3) Keep your home maintained. Poorly maintained properties and neighborhoods are a breeding ground for criminal activity.

▸ **Take self-defense classes.** I don't suggest trying to take on an intruder as a first resort. Prevention and avoidance are my preferred options. But if you are put in the position of having to physically defend yourself, it's good to know (and have practiced!) some kick-ass moves to get you out of a tight squeeze. At best, you'll be able to incapacitate your intruder. At the least you might be able to break their hold long enough to get away and run. Not only are classes good for self-defense, but a bonus side effect might be losing a little weight and getting into shape. That's a win-win in my book!

I think now is the time to address the elephant in the room: the subject of having weapons for self-defense. Let me start by saying that this is in no way intended to be a commentary on the gun control or a $2^{nd}$ Amendment debate. There are valid arguments on both sides, so let's look at this topic simply from a living-alone-safety point of view. There will be times you may wish you had a weapon when prowlers decide to inspect your backyard at 2 a.m. But there are important factors to consider when deciding whether or not to introduce a gun into your home environment. Here are a few:

1. Have an honest look at your tendencies in panicked, stressful situations. Don't think about what you should do, or what you think you would do. Neither you nor I are Superman or Lara Croft. Are you the kind of person who has trouble dialing a phone in a life-or-death situation? Or are you cool as a cucumber in all

situations? Are you 100% sure than, when faced with the terror of an intruder in your home, you will have the presence of mind to unlock a gun safe, remove the weapon and ammunition, and load the gun in complete darkness?

2. Same goes for pepper spray. Do you fumble with keys trying to unlock doors when you think someone is after you? If so, are you sure you will manage to spray the intruder instead of your own eyes? It may sound like a scene from a sitcom, but the internet is riddled with stories of pepper spray attempts gone wrong.

3. In regards to clubs or bats or other blunt force weapons, you have to be strong enough to wield said weapon with enough force to make it count. If you are not strong enough to do any real damage, or prevent it from being taken from you, there's the possibility of the intruder taking the weapon and using it against you.

**Dave's Tip:** If people choose to get a gun for the purpose of protecting themselves, they need to know how and when it is appropriate to use it. They also need to check with their local law enforcement agency on what laws are in effect for that area BEFORE getting the gun. And worth mentioning – a real gun should not be purchased with the idea that merely showing it to someone would be a deterrent. If you aren't willing to use the gun, you've introduced the gun into a situation where there wasn't one before…and many hardened criminals are not as afraid of guns as you'd think.

**Final thoughts from Dave:** Professional criminals dislike: 1) time, 2) noise, 3) light.

TIME: Most thieves like to be into a house in less than 15 seconds; if a criminal needs more than that he probably won't break into your house. This tells us that good quality, re-enforced doors and windows with heavy duty locks are an answer.

LIGHT: If you keep the area around your house well lit (sensor lights are good and inexpensive, too) this will help greatly.

NOISE: Even a small, alert dog, while not intimidating to most people, is a problem to a burglar – he does not want to hear that barking!

This chapter is not meant to scare anyone, or place you in a constant state of intruder paranoia. Quite the opposite, actually. It is intended to give you freedom from fear so you can enjoy all the benefits of living alone. The autonomy of solo domesticity is empowering, and a few simple preventative steps can keep you safe while giving you peace of mind. Dave even says that MOST people are good people. Unfortunately, you sometimes can't tell which ones are which. There's no need to be paranoid – just cautious and confident that you've taken steps to ensure your own safety.

So get out there and dare to live without fear. Take this life and make it your own! And start with your own home-safe-home.

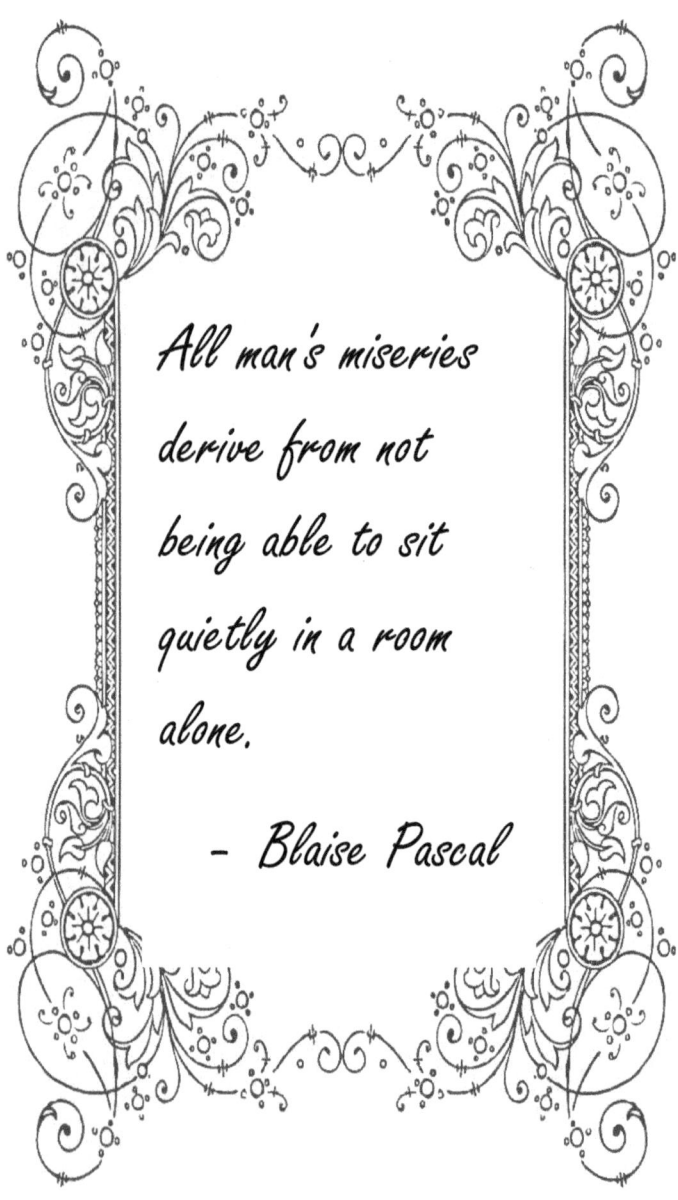

*All man's miseries derive from not being able to sit quietly in a room alone.*

*— Blaise Pascal*

# FURNISHINGS

I recently sold my house and purchased a new one about 90 miles away. By the beach! A dream come true! I absolutely adore it, and couldn't wait to move in. I should have been ecstatic, right? Right!

However, the week before closing, most of my stuff had been moved into storage, and my adorable little house was nearly empty but for a few essentials. And I was inexplicably sad.

As I looked around it struck me…

Sitting in a cold, empty, echoing house is much lonelier than sitting in the same house surrounded by warm memories. My history and who I am as a person at a fundamental level were exactly the same pre- and post-packing. But my comfort, contentedness, and sense of well-being dramatically shifted once my home environment started looking bleak.

And that got me to thinking about how much our home surroundings affect our quality of life, and ultimately our happiness. We subconsciously judge our worth by our surroundings. Or, conversely, let our surroundings mirror our feelings of self-worth. And our environment has a profound effect on our mood. All of this adds up to increased (or decreased) happiness, confidence, and overall outlook.

So, here are my five tips for how to improve your outlook by changing what you look at.

## Tip 1: You Are Worth the Good Stuff

Take a good look at the things you use every day, the things you may take for granted: towels, pots & pans, dishes & utensils, etc. If these things are threadbare, stained, broken, or in some other way sub-par, get rid of them. Being surrounded by old, broken, stained things sends a subconscious message that we are not worth better. Not only is that completely false and unacceptable, it's also unnecessary – even if you're on a tight budget. We live in an age where everyday items are very inexpensive to replace. I'm not talking about spending a gazillion dollars at a luxury store. I'm talking about the ubiquitous discount stores that offer quality items at ridiculously low prices. I've found brand new, good quality towels, pots & pans, and dishware for as little as $2-$3 each. Drying off with a torn, stained, threadbare towel every morning sends the message that we're not worth a new towel. Do yourself a favor and buy new towels. You are worth the investment.

**Tip 2: Discover What Makes You Happy.**

Forget about what the ex-boy/girlfriend or ex-spouse used to like. Forget about the style your parents favored. Just because you liked it 20 years ago, doesn't mean you have to like it forever. (I'm talking to you, country geese wearing blue scarves.) And just because HGTV says it's on-trend doesn't mean you have to have it. (Sorry HGTV – I still love you.) The point is – figure out what you like and what makes you happy, and surround yourself with those things. If a cluttered environment makes you stressed, pack away the knick-knacks and pictures and leave your horizontal surfaces blissfully unadorned. If looking at sparse spaces makes you feel lonely – load 'em up with things that bring you joy. Don't be afraid to be brutally honest. You might think you are a modern millennial and should therefore embrace a contemporary style. But if antiques and vintage make your heart flutter – embrace it! Your home is your sanctuary, and should be filled with things that make you smile.

## Tip 3: Surround Yourself with Wonderful Memories.

Remember that teddy bear your ex-boyfriend won for you at the county fair two years ago? You know, the one you haven't thrown away because you had such a great time with him…before he smashed your heart into a million pieces by sleeping with your coworker? Get. Rid. Of. It. So, you had a great time at the fair. So what? All the negative messages the bear subconsciously taunts you with aren't worth that one good memory. Instead, start making new happy memories for yourself. Don't wait for another significant other to start making memories – get out there and make them for yourself! Treat yourself to a trip somewhere and bring home something that will always remind you of that experience. Take an art or sculpting class and fill your space with your own creativity. Haunt thrift stores and find things that make your heart sing. Cultivate a library of memories, and then fill your space to reflect them.

## Tip 4: Cleanliness Is Next to…Happiness?

We've all felt it – that feeling of calm when we walk into a clean home, versus the feeling of anxiety when we walk into a messy one. Those feelings are real and can have a big impact on our lives. Research shows a direct correlation between the cleanliness of our homes and our overall health and happiness. In a very simplistic, paraphrased explanation, this is because clean homes evoke a sense of harmony, whereas messy homes instill a sense of chaos. And those feelings of harmony/chaos stay with us and infuse every other area of our lives. Being clean and organized isn't the panacea that will cure all our single-person angst and lead us to unending happiness – but it is a key piece in the serenity puzzle.

Here's the problem when it comes to singles; Most single people I know live in apartments that tend to be on the small side. After all, when you're living alone, why pay extra for unneeded space? But small spaces show clutter more easily than large spaces. Additionally – when you're living alone, it's very tempting to let things go because there's no one around to judge or complain. So, chairs become clothes racks, beds become repositories for unfolded laundry, and sinks become storage units for last night's (or last week's) dishes.

The trick is to get in the habit of taking care of things real-time. Get into the "touch-it-only-once" habit.

This means dealing with things as they happen, instead of putting them aside to deal with later. Fold and put away laundry as soon as it comes out of the dryer (one touch) instead of piling the clean laundry onto a bed or chair with the intention of folding it later (two touches). Sort and deal with mail as soon as you bring it in (one touch) instead of piling it on the table to go through later (two or more touches). Although we all have good intentions to address all those "later" chores, the reality is that we get distracted, we lose motivation, or we get busy, and those chores are never completed. The result is that we can't find our favorite shirt, we don't have any clean cereal bowls in the morning, our vehicle registration paperwork gets misplaced, and we can't find the remote. When we start and end our day in frustration and chaos, how can we expect the in between times to be productive and stress-free?

Here are a few more tricks to help get you started on the road to organizational bliss:

1) De-clutter: Sort through your stuff and be brutally honest about your clothes, shoes, and other belongings. Keep only the things you treasure and donate the rest, which makes more room for storage. You can lighten your clutter-load by making it easier to store the stuff you really love.

2) Use a cleaning or organization app: In my book,

*Four Extra Hours*, I detail several cleaning and organization apps that will help you get your life in order.

3) Start small: If cleaning and organizing is a new thing for you, take baby steps. Start by dedicating 30 minutes a day to cleaning and play the "how much can I get done in 30 minutes" game with yourself. Or, start with one task or category (sorting clothes, doing dishes, shredding old paperwork, etc.). Before you know it, your home will be a Zen oasis.

4) Get inspired: Visit home organization sites like apartmenttherapy.com or Pinterest to remind yourself how wonderful it feels to exist in a clean and organized space. A little inspiration can go a long way toward action and implementation.

**Tip 5: Lighten the Mood.**

Recent studies have shown that lighting has a profound effect on mood and productivity. Ever wonder why modern offices are light and bright, and often full of natural light? Light, bright spaces with plenty of natural light boost productivity, increase optimism, and enhance mood. In contrast, darker spaces have a muting effect on mood, and induces feelings of lethargy. There's even a clinical disorder, called Seasonal Affective Disorder (with the apt acronym SAD), linked to the reduction of natural light in winter months, which is characterized by depression, sluggishness, and moodiness.

Unfortunately, large windows are often in short supply in most apartments, so natural light is scarce. In fact, many apartments don't even have room lights, and require their tenants to supply their own lighting in the form of floor or table lamps. So it is imperative to improve your home's lighting situation as part of your overall living-alone strategy. Here are a couple suggestions…

1) Lamps at retail stores can be extremely expensive. Consider haunting local thrift and consignment stores to find lighting solutions at affordable prices. Be sure to check it at the store to make sure it works before taking it home. And if you don't like the shade, don't let that stop you from buying it. Shades can be easily changed, and new, modern shades are plentiful and inexpensive.

2) Look for light bulbs that mimic natural light. Even the new LED bulbs have versions that emit a warm natural light, instead of the blueish light of cheaper fluorescents. And, bonus – LED bulbs are super energy efficient and give off almost no heat.

**Tip 4: Take Time To Smell the Roses…or the Lavender.**

One area of home furnishings that is often overlooked is the air – or, more precisely, what's in the air. The air in your home, the air you breathe, is one of the things that could have the greatest impact on your physical and mental health. Infusing the air of your home with beneficial elements could be the missing piece of your total home health strategy.

Aromatherapy has been used for physical and mental health for many thousands of years. But its use has seen a resurgence in the past 30 years, with new practitioners rediscovering the benefits of these centuries-old therapies. Aromatherapy is a bit of a misnomer because it is about more than just a smell. It is the use of essential oils to affect portions of the brain to trigger healing. This can be done through inhaling, applying directly to the skin, and sometimes even ingesting.

So, how does it work? According to the University of Maryland Medical Center, when essential oils are diffused into the air, the molecules stimulate portions of the brain that affect physical and mental health. There are a wide variety of oils that have a number of uses, including to improve mood, promote relaxation, reduce stress and anxiety, alleviate pain, promote healing, and many more.

The best way to incorporate aromatherapy into your life is to contact a reputable consultant, preferably one who also sells high-quality oils, such as dōTERRA. Your consultant will work with you to discuss what you'd like to address, and the best treatment approach.

Modern-day research around aromatherapy and the use of essential oils is still limited. But there are countless anecdotal reports of the benefits essential oils, and thousands of years of use speak to its enduring popularity. So it's worth a look as one part of your total living-alone strategy.

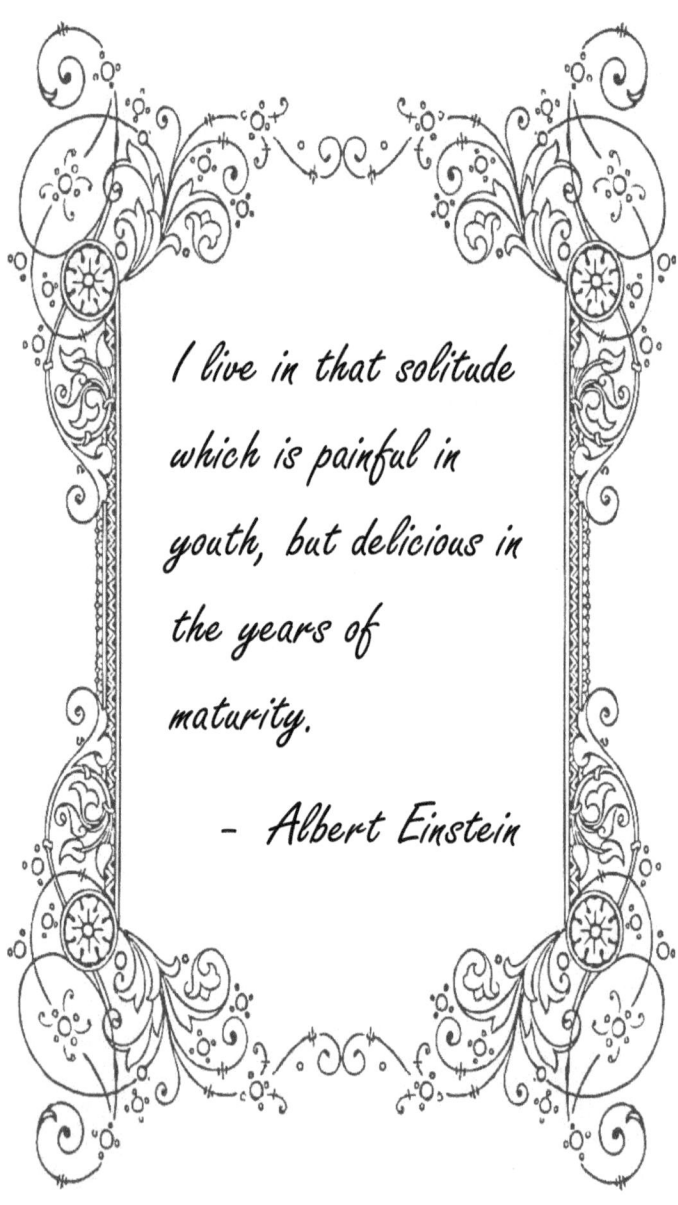

*I live in that solitude which is painful in youth, but delicious in the years of maturity.*

*— Albert Einstein*

# 5

# **GROCERY SHOPPING**

If there's one thing I hate, it's wasting money. As a single person trying to pay a mortgage, manage bills, and enjoy a quality life on one income (in Southern California, no less – one of the most expensive places in the U.S. to live!), I have to make every penny count. And that's why what I'm going to say about grocery shopping is going to sound completely contradictory.

When it comes to buying groceries, less is not always

more. But more is not always more either. Here's what I mean…

When buying food, many economists will tell you to look at the per-unit, or per-ounce price to find the best deal. The lower the per-unit price, the better the deal. And that might be true for families or multi-person households.

But for singles, things are different. We must also factor in whether we'll be able to eat what we buy before it goes bad. Frequently, the individually-packed, single-serving options are more cost effective in the long run, even though there is more upfront cost.

Let's use cottage cheese as an example. A 16-ounce container of cottage cheese costs $3.29, which is $0.21 per ounce. The same 16 ounces of cottage cheese packaged in four individual "On The Go" containers costs $3.99, or $0.25 per ounce. It costs $0.70 more to purchase the same 16 ounces of cottage cheese if purchased in the single-serve packs. When multiplied by numerous items in your shopping cart, it's easy to see how fast it adds up, and why in many cases it is economically smarter to buy in bulk. But not always.

But here's the problem. Buying in bulk, or even standard quantities, is only economical if you're the kind of person who can eat an entire tub of cottage cheese in just a few days. If that's you, go nuts! But if you're like me, and it takes you a few weeks to work through 16 ounces of cottage cheese, there's a big problem. An open container of cottage cheese will only stay fresh in the fridge for about a week. And I'm lucky if I can get through half of it before it goes bad, which means I end up throwing away half the tub. So now the once-inexpensive $3.29 tub of 16 ounces has turned into a very expensive $3.29 tub of 8 ounces, or $0.41 per ounce. Ouch! Since the individually-packaged cottage cheese packs remain sealed in the fridge, they last much, much longer and end up being the economically responsible choice.

So, the moral of that story is to be realistic about your eating habits. Save where you can, but also look for single-serve packaging – you just might reduce food waste and save money in the long-run.

But what do you do with foods that don't come packaged for the single person? Here's a list of my top 10 suggestions for storing bulk food.

**Chicken Breasts:** Before placing chicken breasts in the freezer, I repackage them into individual zip-top freezer bags. This way I can thaw one at a time (if I'm cooking for just me), or two or more if I have guests.

**Ground Beef:** The smallest quantity of pre-packaged

ground beef you can buy is typically one pound. So, unless I'm planning to cook for a group, I break out the ground beef into quarter-pound pieces, flatten them into patties, and place in zip-top bags to go in the freezer. When they're frozen as thin patties, they thaw quickly, which makes cooking much more convenient.

**Hamburger/Hot Dog Buns:** Hamburger and hot dog buns are usually sold in 8-count packs. I've found that hamburger and hot dog buns freeze very well. (Are you seeing a freezer trend here?) However, with these goodies I don't go through the hassle of separating them into individual zip-top bags. I just place the whole package in the freezer. They break apart very easily and thaw quickly.

**Pasta:** A serving size of most pastas is 2 ounces, and there are usually 7 or 8 servings per box of pasta. That's a lot of pasta for one person! Since air and moisture are the main enemies of an open box of pasta, I transfer my unused pasta to a double-storage solution in an attempt to keep out as much air and humidity as possible. First, I transfer the pasta to a zip-top bag and squeeze out as much air as possible. Then I place the sealed pasta into an air-tight glass container. Stored this way, your pasta should last many weeks.

**Pasta Sauce:** A serving size of pasta sauce is ½ cup,

and a regular-sized jar of pasta sauce usually has 6 servings. Luckily, acidic foods last longer in the fridge than non-acidic foods, so it is safe to put the lid back on the glass jar and save it in your fridge for 5-6 days. (Be sure to check it – if it looks off or smells off, don't tempt fate. If in doubt, throw it out.) If I reach day 6 and still haven't used the rest of the jar, I'll use it to make one of my go-to pasta freezer meals, like cheese-stuffed pasta shells, and prolong its life in the freezer. You can find many of these recipes on my website asinglegirlsguideto.com.

**Bananas:** I love bananas. Regular bananas are not wrapped or bundled in the store, so it's easy to pull off two or three from a larger bunch, and purchase only what you know you'll eat. But I always buy organic, which are bundled together and bound with tape in groups of 5-7. Unfortunately, I can usually only eat one a day, which means there are at least 2 or 3 bananas that turn brown before I can eat them. If they do, I will peel them, slice them into half-inch chunks, and freeze them in zip-top bags. Frozen bananas are great in smoothies. Or, place the frozen banana pieces, plus a bit of cocoa or peanut butter or honey & cinnamon into a blender to make "nice cream" (faux ice cream). And, of course, there is always banana bread.

**Bread:** I love bread, but I can rarely go through an entire loaf before the last quarter of it dries out or starts turning funny colors. My local store used to carry half loaves, which were perfect for me! But sadly those were discontinued. Storing bread in the fridge instead of on the counter top prolongs its life by double. And, bread also does surprisingly well in the freezer. Take it out piece-by-piece as you need it. Slices thaw quickly with just a few seconds in the toaster. But be careful not to keep it in the freezer too long. The moisture in bread makes it susceptible to freezer burn.

**Butter:** Unless I'm baking for the holidays, or in recipe-testing mode for one of my cookbooks, butter seems to languish in my fridge for long periods of time. Butter is one of those things that quickly absorbs odors from other foods, so it's not long before I have onion-scented butter. Good for sautéing potatoes – not so good on toast. One trick for keeping butter fresh in the fridge is to buy the type that is wrapped in foil, like Kerrygold Irish Butter. The foil keeps out the other fridge smells, and the butter stays sweet-tasting longer. And, of course, you can always store sticks of butter in the freezer until you're ready to use them.

**Cereal:** There are few things I hate more than stale cereal. But, unless I've recently treated myself to a box of Cap'n Crunch, it takes a long, long time for me to work through an entire box of cereal. Their cardboard box and plastic bag packaging don't do a great job of keeping the contents fresh once they're opened. To minimize the staling effects of ambient air and humidity, I pour the boxed cereal into air-tight Rubbermaid or Tupperware containers. These containers are specifically made for cereal, with a hand-hold on one side and a pour spout on the other. They won't keep your Cap'n Crunch fresh indefinitely, but will make it last much longer than its original packaging.

**Cheese:** If you've read my recipes, you know how I feel about pre-shredded cheese. Pre-shredded cheese is coated with a substance that prevents the shreds from clumping together. In taste-tests, that coating can be detected, and can affect the way it melts. So I always, always (did I mention always?) buy my cheese in bricks, and then grate it as needed. But that means I often have bricks of cheese that run the risk of going bad in my fridge. The solution? You guessed it…freeze it! Yes – cheese can freeze! The harder the cheese, the better it freezes and re-thaws. Cut it into pieces no larger than half a pound, wrap it in plastic wrap, then place it in a zip-top bag, and into the freezer. A word of warning here: Freezing changes the texture of cheese. When it thaws it's still great for cooking and melting, but I wouldn't slice it for a cheese and cracker tray at your next party. Save the fresh stuff for that.

Saving money is an ongoing challenge for everyone,

but is particularly important for those trying to survive on one income. Preventing food waste is a big part of that process. With a little resourcefulness and creativity, grocery shopping can become part of your solo lifestyle saving plan rather than spending plan.

I only go out to get me a fresh appetite for being alone.

— Lord Byron

# COOKING

Cooking. It's funny how one word can encompass so many of the not-so-pleasant aspects of living alone. Recipes are usually geared toward feeding a family of four or more. It's hard to justify dirtying up all those dishes just for yourself. And contrary to some married people's opinion – single people have very busy lives too, and cooking takes time that we just don't have.

It all seems like an exercise in futility, doesn't it? I'd rather just go through the drive-thru on the way home from work.

Or would I?

The average fast food meal is full of preservatives and sodium and fat and sugar and ultra-processed ingredients. A steady diet of the stuff can potentially cause serious health issues. And, while an individual fast-food meal doesn't seem to take a big chunk out of your wallet, especially since most fast-food chains are adding value menus to their dining options, adding up a week's worth of meals causes quite a financial dent.

This is where cooking could save the culinary day.

Cooking your own food gives you total control over what you're eating. You can use whole foods, organic ingredients, and limit the amount of salt and sugar that's added. Additionally, if you're smart about how you shop and use leftovers, cooking at home is a big money saver in the long run. But I didn't need to type any of those things because you already knew all that. And even though those are very important benefits of cooking at home, they don't address the real issues of the task: the drudgery and difficulty of cooking for one.

So here are some ideas to kick-start your career as a solo culinary guru. And bonus: most of these tips translate to cooking for two or for a family, should that need ever arise.

- Subscribe to websites that specialize in recipes for one or two. Many of the well-known food industry names and television programs have a whole category of recipes geared towards singles. Or, if you prefer to have recipes in paper form, subscribe to a cooking-for-two magazine, and practice halving the recipes. I've tried a whole host of recipes from both sources. Many are hits, but a few are misses, so you may have to do your own testing to find the sites and recipes you like.

- Use a slow cooker. As a single person working a full time job (and often two jobs), my slow cooker has become one of my best friends. I have a small one that's perfect for single meals, and a larger one for when I'm expecting guests. I also have a whole host of cookbooks for slow cookers, and at least a half dozen cooking sites that specialize in slow cooker meals. They're the workhorse of my kitchen, because they require so little effort. I just put the ingredients in before I leave for work, turn the cooker on, and I dinner is ready and waiting for me when I get home. And bonus: the slow cooker offers two additional benefits; 1) it does not heat up the house like the oven does, and 2) it is economical because it can turn an inexpensive piece of meat into a melt-in-your-mouth gourmet meal.

- Become an expert in one-pot meals. One of the most dreaded parts of cooking is the clean-up. I know I've been guilty of not wanting to cook just because I didn't want to do the dishes that would be waiting for me post-dinner. Do yourself a favor and remove that looming chore by creating one-pot meals. Soups and stews are the things most people think about when they think about one-pot meals. But there's so much more! Try creating pot pies, or shepherd's pies, or a pot roast with roasted vegetables, or baked chicken and potatoes, or a casserole – you get the idea. Cooking your main and your side(s) in the same dish or pot usually means easy preparation and minimal clean-up.

- Try new gadgets like the 7-in-1 Instant Pot. I'm not a fan of the uni-tasker. Real estate in my kitchen is scarce and valuable, so whatever appliance lives there has to earn its keep. The Instant Pot is one such tool. This multi-function wonder is super easy to use (once you get past the inevitable intimidation) and can be used to make delicious foods fast. And the best part is that you never have to worry about what to do when you forget to thaw your frozen meats. The Instant Pot (or, IP for us Instant Pot junkies), handles frozen foods like a champ. The nice thing about this feature is that my world of food prep is no longer limited by time or temperature. There are other gadgets on the market like this, so do a little homework and see what makes sense for you. This may be a fad, like the fondue pot (why that ever went out of fashion, I have no idea – there is nothing not good about the fondue pot!), but as far as I'm concerned, the Instant Pot is my new kitchen gadget staple, and it's not going anywhere.

- Meal planning is not just for families anymore. Once a chore relegated to the soccer mom set, the idea of meal planning has grown to include singles. Our lives are getting busier every day, and without a little pre-planning we may have no choice but to swing through the drive-thru. But then, we have to spend an extra hour or two at the gym to work off the burger and fries we just ate. And then we no longer have time to go to the market or to cook, because we spent extra time at the gym, so we opt for the drive-thru again. And then the gym even more… You get the idea – it's a downward spiral of time-wasting gloom. So spend a little time up-front to meal plan for the week. On Saturday or Sunday, take a look at your week ahead. Do you have plans, appointments, days you know you're going to work late, etc? Plan meals accordingly (menus, ingredients, etc.), then take a trip to the market to make sure you have all the ingredients you need.

You might even spend an hour or two Sunday night prepping some make-ahead items. Wash and cut your veggies, make sides that reheat well (I'm thinking about you, mashed potatoes!), or slow-cook that roast that you'll turn into a trio of mouthwatering meals in the coming days. (Steak salad, beef tacos, shepherd's pie, shredded beef quesadillas, shredded BBQ beef sliders, and baked potatoes with beef and broccoli toppings are a few that come to mind.) Taking the guesswork out of cooking makes it a lot less stressful, and a lot more likely that you'll actually do it.

- Make sure your pantry and freezer are stocked with staples. Take a look at the "Grocery" chapter of this book for tips on storing items so they'll last longer. Here's a list of what I usually keep on-hand:

    - Pasta and Sauce
    - Chicken breasts (frozen individually)
    - Ground beef (frozen in ¼ pound patties)
    - Chuck roast
    - Rice
    - Quinoa
    - Frozen veggies
    - Canned beans
    - Chicken and vegetable stock
    - A variety of canned soups
    - A variety of oils

- A variety of spices
- Flour, sugar, corn starch, baking soda/powder
- Pie crusts (frozen)
- Puff pastry (frozen)
- Sweetened condensed milk and evaporated milk
- Chocolate chips
- Fruit (frozen)

With these items, you can make just about anything if you have a last-minute dinner party. And, if you supplement these staples with fresh produce each week, you're golden! Speaking of fresh produce…

☛ Make the local farmer's market part of your weekly routine. Almost every city has one, so make use of it. They are both fun and practical. Get to know your local farmers. Every farmer I've ever met at a market loves to talk about his/her produce and usually has great information on recipes, what's in season, cooking tips, etc. A visit to the farmer's market can be inspirational, get you excited to cook, and keep up your enthusiasm. And bonus: farmer's markets usually offer more than just produce. There are often other vendors selling a variety of fun things. So a mundane shopping trip can turn into a treasure hunting adventure.

- Host regular dinner gatherings. Offer to cook, and have your friends bring desserts or beverages. Using this tactic, you'll be forced to cook, and you will get into the habit (aka more comfortable) preparing meals. Chances are you'll also have leftovers, which you can then turn into other things. Speaking of which...

- Become a leftover guru. It's hard to find recipes for one. So don't be afraid to make more than you can eat, and then find creative ways to use those leftovers. It could be an entirely new meal that has no resemblance to the first, or turning those leftovers into ingredients for soups/stews – let your imagination go! Or, be a little more pragmatic and be intentional about your leftover plans. I used to work two jobs – an office job during the day, and performing at night. That meant I had very little time to do things like sleep. Consequently, I preferred to spend my mornings sleeping as late as possible rather than trying to pack a lunch for my day job. My solution was to cook on Sunday. I'd cook a roast or a chicken and have tons of leftovers. All I had to do then was to repackage those foods into other delicious meals to grab-and-go each morning. My office coworkers were consistently jealous at my delicious-smelling lunches. They were, in my opinion, far superior to a boring brownbag sandwich or the building's cafeteria food, and much cheaper, too!

- Pre-cook individual meals. I will often gather the ingredients for some of my favorite meals, and prep them on a Saturday or Sunday. I buy the disposable mini loaf pans, then make a recipe designed for four and divide it up into the individual pans. I cover them with foil, label them, and put them in the freezer. Then all I have to do when I get home is turn on my oven and throw in whatever I feel like having for dinner that night. Now, you might be thinking, "Can't I do that already with frozen meals in a box from the grocery store?" Well, of course the high-level answer is Yes. But I ask you to think about all the sodium, preservatives, stabilizers, fillers, and who-knows-what-else could be in those meals. By making and freezing them yourself, you know exactly what's in them. Currently in my freezer, I have individual portions of lasagna, mac-and-cheese, meatloaf and mashed potatoes, and shepherd's pie. All are easy to make in bulk, and all heat up beautifully in the oven.

- Start small. If you're not used to cooking for one, or cooking at all for that matter, start by cooking one day a week. Make it a low-stress day, like a Sunday, when you don't have a bunch of other things scheduled so it doesn't become just another thing to dread. Once you get the hang of cooking and meal planning, increase the cooking days to two or three. Continue adding cooking days until you're comfortable. Maybe it's all 7 days. Maybe it's only four or five. I usually have a pretty good idea of what my week entails, so I can make a general game plan on Sunday, do my shopping and some quick prep Sunday night, and be all set for the whole week. Honestly, it doesn't take that much time on Sunday, and the time and money I save during the week more than makes up for it.

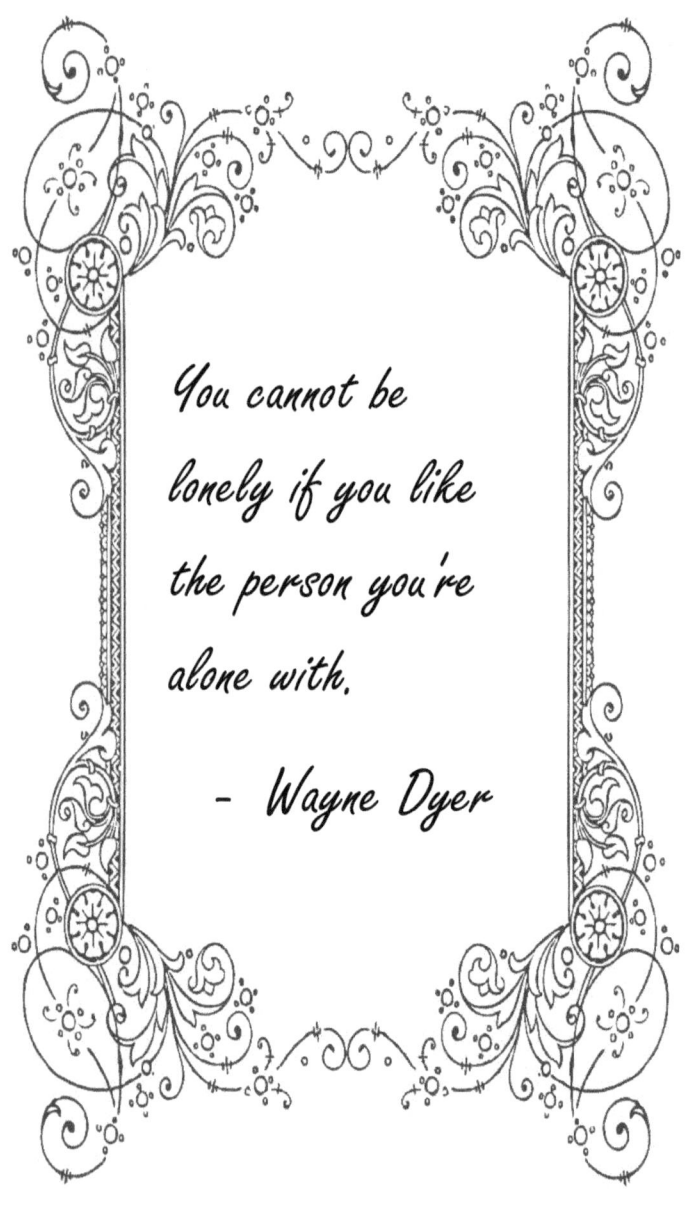

You cannot be lonely if you like the person you're alone with.

- Wayne Dyer

# DINING OUT

Being single doesn't mean I want to eat at home or via a drive-thru all the time. Sometimes, even when I'm date-less, I want to eat in an actual sit-down restaurant. Even a not-so-fancy restaurant will do. Sometimes, I just want to sit at a table and have someone cook and bring me my meal, while I relax and enjoy the experience of dining out.

But eating alone can be terrifying to some and humiliating to others. There seems to be a negative perception or stigma around solo diners. Many singles fear they're being stared at, pitied for their singlehood, or even despised for taking up a perfectly good 2-person or 4-person table just for themselves. We fear that solitary dining is not a sign of our strength, but rather evidence of our lack of friends or social standing. We think we are presenting ourselves as lonely, pathetic figures for people to look down upon. Well, here's the truth. They're not. I promise, no one is looking at you. No one is judging you. I don't mean this harshly, it's just a true statement about society. People spend way too much time convinced that everyone is staring at them, judging them. But the reality is that most people are too absorbed in their own personal world to even notice anyone else in the room. If we actually knew how infrequently people thought about us, we'd stop caring about what it is we think they're thinking.

The fact is, as the rate of singlehood in the United States increases, so too does the percentage of solo diners. A recent national eating study conducted by market research company NPD found that well over 50% of the US population now dines alone. This trend is attributed the shift in demographics. As more people remain (or become) single, the stigma of dining alone is slowly fading, and the number of solo diners increases. And, according to industry experts, restaurants are responding to this trend by offering more two-seat tables, menu items geared toward individual diners, and faster turnover times (since single diners are unlikely to linger like couples or groups do).

Yet despite these trends, some people still feel awkward sitting at a table for one. The social construct of dining out involves an element of community and shared experience – even if that sharing is only with one other person. To buck that perceived expectation requires a certain amount of chutzpah. So here are a few survival tips that will give you the confidence to dine alone with pride and without an ounce of shame.

- 🍽 Bring a book or magazine to read. Having something to read does a few things. First, it gives us something to do in the absence of conversation. Second, it gives us a reason not to notice anyone that might happen to look our way. Third, it gets us out of our head, and prevents us from unnecessarily worrying about what people are thinking. And finally, it creates for us an invisible barrier which helps us feel less vulnerable.

- 🍽 Bring your laptop, or a notebook and pens/pencils. No one knows if you are a famous author, or a successful business person in town for a conference, or a venture capitalist looking for the next big thing. And that's the beauty of dining alone – no one knows who you are or why you're there. So if you're worried about perception, adopt a role for the evening and use your props to support your character. And bonus: if you really are an author, or ever wanted to be one, you could actually use that time to write – like I'm doing right now.

- 🍽 Do NOT feel guilty about sitting at a table alone. Chances are the host or hostess will seat you at a 2-person table anyway, so it's not like you're taking up any "extra" seating space. But even if you were seated at a larger table, fight the urge to feel guilty or conspicuous! The reality is that solo diners generally eat faster than couples or groups, so the table will turn over quickly, and the fact that you've had the gall (gasp!) to sit solo at a table will not cause any significant slow-down in seating speed or income earned. However...

- 🍽 If you just can't shake that uncomfortable feeling of having a table all to yourself, start small by choosing a seat at the bar or at a communal table. Many restaurants are now catering to solo diners by increasing their number of bar-type seating and communal tables. Having these dining options completely removes any stigma of sitting alone because the *expectation* is that you are dining alone.

- 🍽 Tip generously – even if you're sitting at the bar. It takes nearly as much work to wait on solo diners as it does to serve a table of two or four, but the dinner check is much smaller. Consequently, the wait staff make less on tips. Make up for that discrepancy by being generous with your gratuity.

- Do a little reconnaissance before being seated. Check the place out to feel the vibe. If there are other solo diners, or if it's a laid-back place, you're good to go. But if you feel a negative vibe, don't be afraid to leave and go somewhere else. Chances are, you'd get that same negative vibe even if you were there with a group, and no one needs negativity when dining out.

- Learn to like your own company. It's often awkward to eat alone because we just don't know what to do with ourselves without someone across the table to act as our conversational foil. If this is you, distract yourself by playing imagination games. Take a cue from road trip games, and come up with your own form of dining alone games. Make up stories about your fellow restaurant patrons and how they connect with each other – like your own version of *Murder on the Orient Express*. Play "cliché" bingo, and listen to see how many cliché phrases you hear spoken around you. Notice all the details of the room – the art on the walls, the architecture, the decorative touches – and imagine where they came from and if they had a "life" before adorning that restaurant. After a few outings you'll find you don't need these distraction games, and you can just relax and enjoy the restaurant experience.

- Accept that not every dining out experience is going to be an exercise in singlehood kick-assery. Sometimes it's going to suck. Sometimes you're going to make a tactical error and find yourself in a romantic restaurant alone on Valentine's Day. (Not that I'm speaking from experience here.) But with anything, the more you do it, the more confident you'll become and the more fun you'll have. And once you're relaxed you can fully enjoy all the perks of flying solo.

- Take baby steps. If you're not ready for dinner – the big league of solo dining – start smaller. Go out to breakfast or lunch, or just for coffee. Breakfast, lunch, and snack times are far less intimidating than dinner, so use those meals to get comfortable with the prospect before jumping into the deep end of solo dining.

- Take something to use as a seat saver. When you're with a friend or group, you don't have to worry about your table being cleared and re-seated while you're in the restroom. But when you're solo – a quick trip to the loo could mean an unexpectedly early end to your meal. So take a sweater or scarf or something to leave draped over your chair just in case you need to go to the restroom mid-meal.

- Be open to conversation – if you feel like it. Your server might just have a fantastic sense of humor, or really funny stories to tell. Let yourself stay open to the possibility of conversation should the opportunity present itself. It takes courage and bravery to chit-chat with a total stranger. But you could be the positivity the server really needed that day, or it could be the start of a beautiful friendship.

- And finally, if you are absolutely sure that everyone is looking at you and noticing your single status, bring something to make them wish they were you. Take a bunch of travel brochures to exotic locations and make notes as if you're planning your next great adventure. Onlookers will envy your exciting life. Take a highlighted script and "learn your lines" during dinner. Gawkers will wonder who you are and what movie or TV show you're in. Put a fun cover on whatever book you're reading – maybe one that says "You've Just Won the Lottery – Now What Do You Do?" That'll keep 'em guessing! But I promise you – none of these gimmicks will be needed, because no one is judging you anyway.

The moral of the story is this: don't let singlehood prevent you from having a nice meal at a full-on, sit-down, table-service restaurant. Get out there and enjoy all the food and the service you want without a second thought to your solo status. You deserve it. We all do.

Only one question remains. What's for dinner?

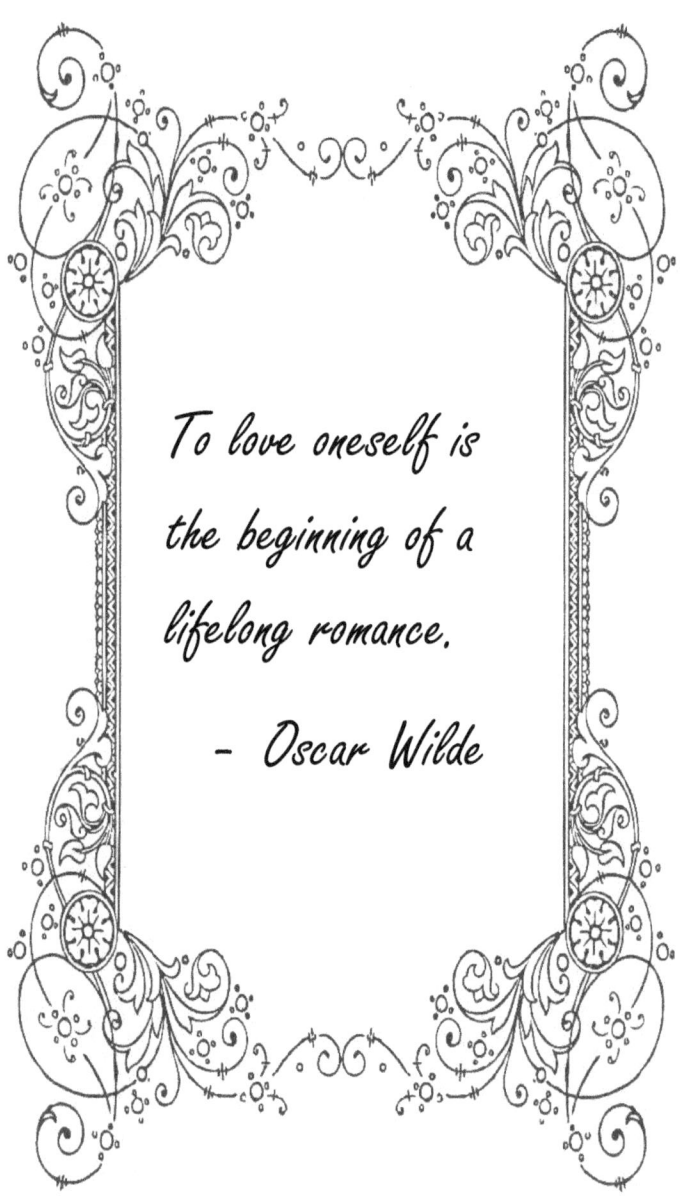

To love oneself is the beginning of a lifelong romance.

— Oscar Wilde

# SLEEPING

Important note: In this chapter, when I use the word "sleeping" I mean actually sleeping, not *wink-wink-nudge-nudge* sleeping.

OK – now that we've gotten that out of the way…

Sleeping with a spouse or partner is one of the most intimate things a couple can do. You trust another person to lay next to you while you're asleep – one of a person's most vulnerable and helpless states. Not to mention allowing them to see you in the morning with sleepy eyes and bed hair and morning breath.

For singles, nighttime and sleeping alone can be the most challenging parts of flying solo. There's something about the night that amplifies loneliness. During the day, there's light, there's hope, there are people around, there's activity and noise and life. But at night, the darkness closes in and we feel isolated and alone.

I have never been married, and I don't have long-term experience of what it's like to share a bed with someone, and then have to navigate nights without them. So I asked my married and formerly married friends, in addition to my single friends, to participate in an informal survey about the positives and negatives of sharing the covers, and how they coped when they were suddenly sleeping alone.

Nearly everyone who participated agreed there are pros and cons on both sides of the bed-sharing issue. Some people prefer to sleep alone – even some married couples preferred separate beds and even separate rooms. When you sleep alone, you don't have to worry about snoring, someone stealing the blanket, a bed hog, or someone breathing on you. You have the freedom to move around and sleep any way you want, without being woken up by your partner's snooze alarm going off again. And again. And again.

An overwhelming majority, however, said they preferred sharing their bed with a special someone, and found it more difficult to sleep alone. Most women reported feeling safer when their spouse was with them, and that their spouse helped keep them warm. One of the most surprising things to me was that both men and women reported "pillow talk" as one of their favorite things about sleeping together. It is that connection, that time where the world shrinks to just you two, that reaffirms the intimate connection and partnership.

I also asked my friends to share with me how they coped when they had to sleep alone. Following is a list of tips and tricks I and/or my friends employ to make those long, lonely nights a little more bearable.

- Surround yourself with positivity. (See chapter 9.) If you go to bed with positive feelings, you're less likely to be ambushed by the negative ones once you crawl into bed.

- Establish your own bedtime rituals. Take care of your skin by washing your face and applying a good night time moisturizer (yes – even if you're a guy). Take care of your teeth (brush and floss). Set out your clothes for the next day, etc. Having a regular ritual gets your brain into sleep mode faster, leaving you less time to fret about being alone.

- ✓ Take a cue from the movie *Something's Gotta Give* and sleep in the middle of the bed. If you don't have a "side," you're not constantly reminded that no one has the other side.

- ✓ To reassure your safety, check all door locks and window locks. Most people I know are pretty good about checking door locks, but completely forget about windows. If you have an alarm system, make sure it's activated. Make this a part of your bedtime ritual.

- ✓ If you're used to sleeping with another body in the bed with you, prop up pillows under the blanket, so when you roll over in the middle of the night, you won't be startled by the absence of a body.

- ✓ Make bedtime a sacred time. Tap into your faith or spiritual beliefs by reading, praying, memorizing verses, or practicing meditation.

- ✓ Have some "go to" happy movies or TV shows at the ready. These, combined with your TV's sleep timer, can be one way of getting past the fear of being alone at night.

- ✓ Try a weighted blanket. These are blankets

specially designed to help people with anxiety, depression, PTSD, etc. The extra weight is comforting and makes us feel safe and secure. Additionally, the touch of pressure provided by its weight encourages the body's production of serotonin, which promotes better sleep.

- If you have a pet, let the pet sleep in bed with you. It's amazing how much heat those little bodies produce when they sleep. Also, just the presence of another living thing sharing your space is comforting and helps us feel not so alone.

- If you suffer from nightmares, not having someone next to you to comfort you can be a huge downside to sleeping alone. Keep a pad of paper and pencil by your bed. When you wake up from a nightmare, write down as many details as you can remember. The process of writing them down will help clear your head. Then in the light of day, read through your notes and try to analyze your dream. Many psychologists believe dreams are our subconscious minds' way of working through issues. If we can work through the issues in our conscious minds during the day, those nightmares may go away.

- Since solo sleepers don't have anyone to share "pillow talk" with, do your own form of singles pillow talk by keeping a gratitude journal. Before you go to bed each night, write a list of 10 things you were thankful for that day. Some nights it might be a stretch to get to 10. Other nights your list will be 20 or 30 items long. Focusing on the positives of the day puts our minds in a happy place, which is more conducive to sleep.

- If you're used to your spouse's sleeping (or snoring), and it's too quiet to sleep without it, try a white noise app on your phone or alarm clock. The sounds of rainstorms and the ocean are my favorite – just beware of the seagulls.

- Leave a light on in the house, or have a nightlight in your room. Having a space that's not completely pitch-black makes it a little less scary if you hear something go bump in the night.

- Indulge in a little sleep luxury. Splurge on the super high thread count sheets. Give yourself the gift of the plush comforter, or exquisite memory foam mattress topper. Treat yourself like the queen or king of your castle that you are. If your bed is glorious enough, you'll look forward to climbing into it, regardless of whether there's someone to share it with you or not.

Nighttime can be the most difficult aspect of living alone. For some, it's an overwhelming feeling of loss. For some, it's the reminder of a wish unfulfilled. It's not so much the presence of an empty space, it's the lack of presence in the space. And when the loneliness is combined with the fear of being alone, sleepless nights are the inevitable result.

But by being intentional about our evening mindset and pre-bed rituals, it is possible to flip that switch from negative nighttime to serene slumber.

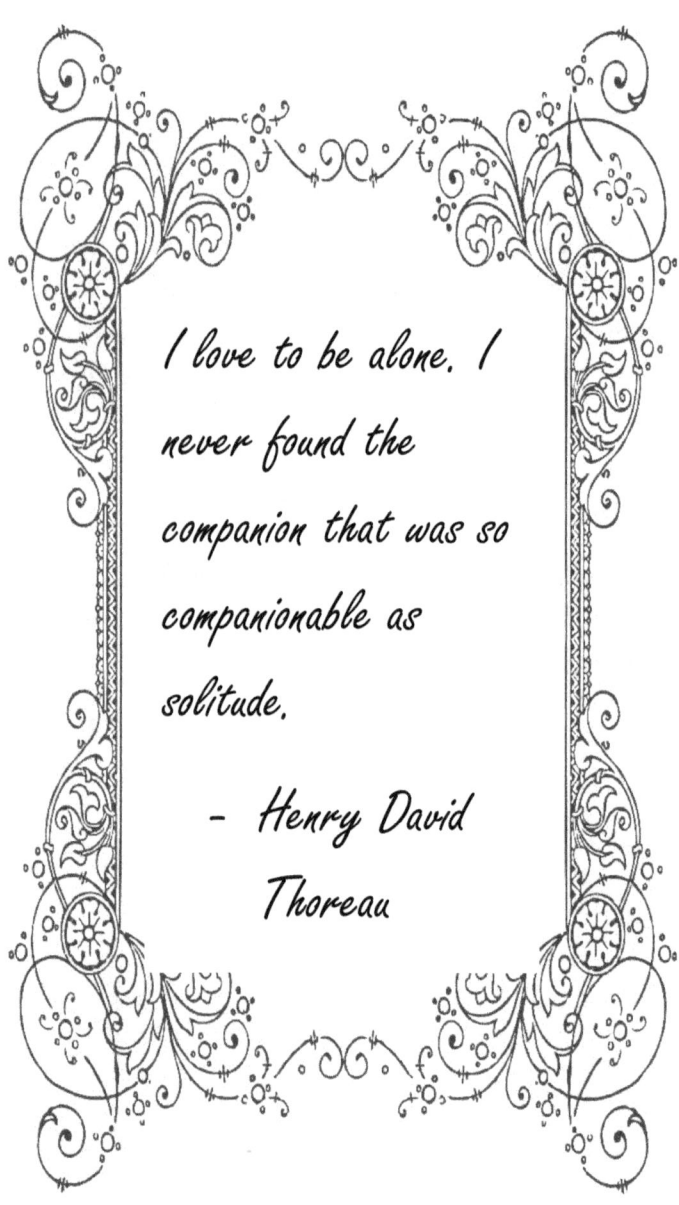

*I love to be alone. I never found the companion that was so companionable as solitude.*

*- Henry David Thoreau*

# SOCIAL LIFE

This may seem like an odd topic for an entire chapter. After all, isn't that one of the biggest perks of being single and living alone? You can have a busy and full social life without the complications of another person's needs and demands. You have complete freedom. You have complete autonomy. You can go out anytime you want and stay out as late as you'd like without worrying about getting a sitter. You can do all the things your married mommy/daddy friends only dream of. So what's the problem?

Well, there's Netflix. And a comfy couch. And yoga pants. Need I go on?

The idea of going out and the reality of going out are often two very different things. The idea of going out is being all spiffed up and looking good, mingling with other people who look good, having a lot of laughs while sipping delicious drinks and nibbling amazing food. The reality of going out means having to shower and do your hair, put on something other than yoga pants, deal with traffic, find parking, then sit awkwardly with people you may or may not know and just hope and pray you don't say something that will make you look stupid.

Ugh. Never mind. Someone hand me the remote.

Kidding. (Sort of.)

The truth of our biology is that we are social beings – pack animals, if you will. We are hardwired to crave social interaction, physical touch, and emotional connection with other humans. And when we live alone, we lack those elements that are an innate part of our being. But that doesn't mean we *have* to live with someone in order to be happy. There is a big difference between social isolation and choosing to live alone. We can fulfill those elemental needs and find happiness, even in solo domesticity.

Most people prefer going places and doing things with other people. I know I do. But in the absence of available friends and family, you don't have to sit at home alone and mope. (Although, to be honest, sometimes that does feel easier.) No – instead, learn to have fun by yourself. It takes a lot more motivation to get out and do things by yourself. But once you learn to have fun and find happiness on your own terms, without relying on another person, you have regained power over your own happiness. And no one can ever take that away from you.

Here are some ways to have an active and vital social life, even if you live alone.

- **Join groups with shared interests.** One of the easiest and least awkward ways of getting involved in social activities is to seek out those with similar interests. After all, you already have a built-in conversation starter! There are groups that focus on nearly every interest and hobby imaginable: hiking groups, political organizations, book clubs, craft guilds, support groups, conservation corps, booster/fundraising clubs, and many more – too many to list. Figure out where your passions lie, then seek out those groups.

- **Participate in community events.** Every city, town, state, and even neighborhood host events throughout the year. Find the keeper of your local calendar, or subscribe to your local chamber of commerce calendar, to learn about the goings-on near you. Not only will your attendance support your community, you'll get to know your neighbors in the process.

- **Enlist a friend.** We've already established that it's more fun to go places and do things with other people, so make it happen. Enlist a friend to be your cohort, your partner in crime, the other half of your dynamic duo, the Thelma to your Louise (but skip the driving off a cliff part). It doesn't have to be a single friend. Many of my mommy-friends would love to get out and hang with adults if the barriers to doing so were removed. So offer to pay for childcare, if that's an obstacle. Find free things to do (there are a ton of 'em) if finances are an issue. Or find kid/dog friendly activities. The point is that where there's a will there's a way. And it will do you both good to get out of the house.

- **Say yes.** Resist the urge to be a hermit. Yeah – it's a pain to get ready, deal with traffic, find parking, and all the other things that go with getting out. But once you do, I'll bet you'll be glad you did. I've found the hardest part of any outing is just deciding to do it, and taking that first step. Once you've done that, once you're committed, you'll find you actually accomplish what you set out to do. So say yes. Say yes to party invitations, to girls' nights out, to game nights, to dinner parties, to dinner and a movie, to drinks and dancing. Say yes to opening your life to opportunity and adventure.

🍀 **Invite people over.** If you don't want to go out to people, bring people in to you. Host a dinner party, game night, barbecue, potluck, book club, whatever. It's fun to have people over, to open your home and share your space with friends. And bonus: it might even inspire you to vacuum or fold that laundry that's been taunting you for days.

🍀 **Take a class.** Even in my little town there are endless opportunities to take classes. And if I drive to the main city, the options are endless. I could take a different class a week for the rest of my life and never repeat one. Investigate the offerings at the local college, adult learning center, community center, or private studios. You'll find classes for all levels in cooking, crafting, art, fitness, dance, music, martial arts, mechanics, home improvement, history, health, finance – there are classes to suit every interest.

🍀 **Volunteer.** Many studies have shown that one key to happiness is to give. And what better way to give than to share your time and talents for a worthy cause? Find an organization that shares your passion, and learn how you can become involved. The great part about volunteering is that it is action-oriented, and everyone has a task to do. So solo participants don't feel awkward to be there alone, because there is always an activity to focus on instead of struggling to make small talk with a complete stranger.

- **Get involved in your church.** Most churches have outreach groups of all varieties. Some are geared toward segments of the population in need of assistance. Some focus on missions. And some simply focus on fellowship and ministry opportunities within their own church family. Last night I had a lot of fun attending a bowling night coordinated by one such group. I knew many of the people there, but certainly not all. It was a fun, no-stress way to get involved, meet new people, and show off my spectacularly bad bowling skills in a supportive and safe environment.

- **If you're a dog owner, get to know your dog parks.** Most cities have them now, and their popularity is on the rise. This is another area where it's perfectly normal and acceptable, even expected, to go to alone. I've been to dozens of dog parks, and most dog owners are there alone (with Fido, of course). These micro communities also offer tons of get-to-know-you opportunities and built-in conversation starters. Which dog is yours? What's his/her name? What kind of dog is he/she? How long have you had him/her? Before you know it, you're having a full conversation with a new dog park friend.

🐾 **Take yourself on a date.** Being social doesn't always mean you have to meet new people, or go out with people you already know. Sometimes it just means being in public where other people already are. One great way to do this is to take yourself on a date. Treat yourself to dinner and a movie. (See the chapter about dining alone, if this idea makes you queasy.) Enjoy a night of theater. (I'm often surprised at how many people attend stag.) Go to a sports bar to watch the game. If you sit at the bar instead of a table, you may be surprised at how easily conversation happens. The point is that almost any outing that is traditionally done as a couple or a group can also be enjoyed as a singleton, if you have the right mindset. So don't let being alone stop you from getting out and doing the things you love.

Living alone is a popular lifestyle choice that is growing in popularity every day. But for optimum emotional health, there needs to be a balance – a balance between having alone time and being chronically alone, between being alone and being lonely. And even though it sometimes feels like a lot more trouble than it's worth, being in the company of other humans is necessary for our overall well-being.

So take a few steps to increase your sociability quotient. It's just like most things – the more you do it, the easier it gets. And the easier it gets, the more fun you'll have. So let your inner social butterfly fly free.

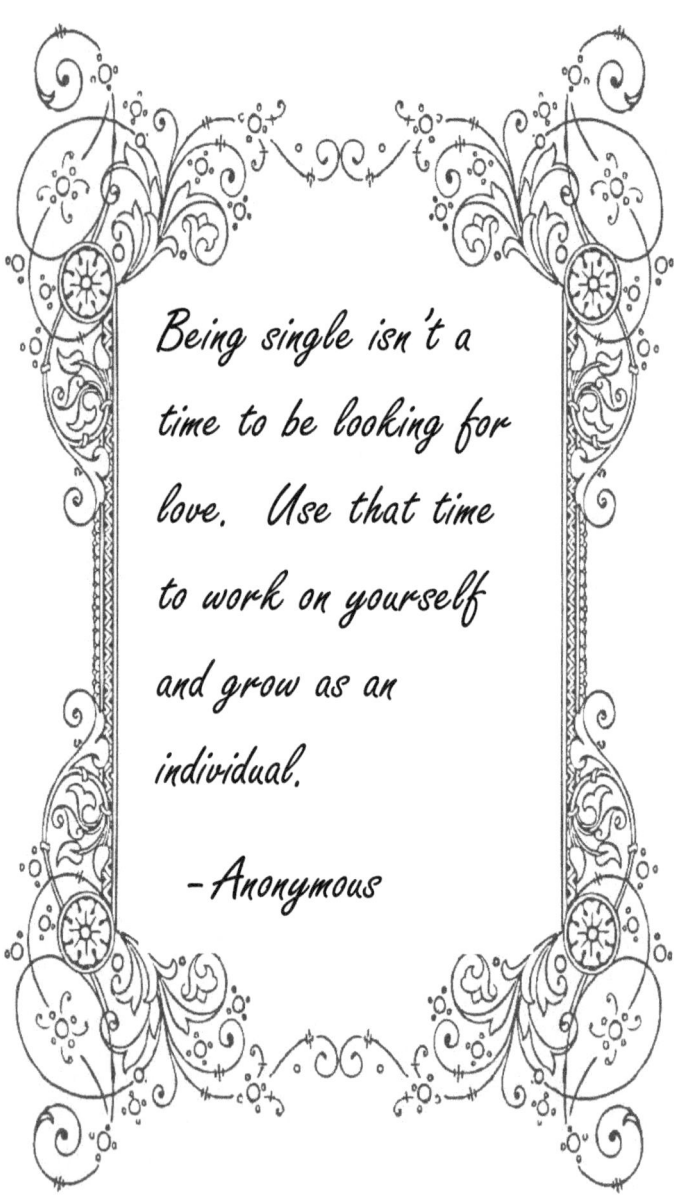

Being single isn't a time to be looking for love. Use that time to work on yourself and grow as an individual.

- Anonymous

# FITNESS

Working out. Ugh. I hate those words.

Just the thought of them makes me want to run in the other direction. (Well, maybe not run, 'cuz that would be too much like *working out*. But you get my drift.) I've never been a gym rat, and I never will be. I've never experienced that "runner's high" or the "workout high" that so many fitness fanatics claim they feel. Personally, I think it's a lie. (Not really.)

But the harsh reality is that we humans need to

exercise. Gone are the days when survival gave us all the exercise we needed. For most of us today, survival means sitting at a desk staring at a computer. Then we're so mentally exhausted at the end of the day, we go home and sit on the couch and stare at a TV. That sedentary lifestyle spells disaster for our health. In fact, doctors say that a sedentary lifestyle is as bad for our health as smoking. Sitting for too long every day, day after day, can lead to heart disease, various cancers, diabetes, high blood pressure, high cholesterol, and a host of other chronic health issues.

Yikes! That's terrifying!

Yet despite the grave consequences of not exercising, the act of actually doing a workout still seems beyond the realm of possibility for most of us. It's such a pain (literally and figuratively) and takes so much time (that none of us have) and is so boring, that a root canal would be preferable to a trip to the gym. OK, maybe it's not *that* bad, but it's close.

If you have a roommate or a spouse or kids, you could enlist them in helping you stay motivated and keeping you accountable. In fact, you could even include them in your workout plans – fitness is for everyone! But if you're single and live alone, you are left to motivate yourself.

Again…ugh. Pass me the remote, Netflix is calling.

But seriously, though – the trick to staying motivated and meeting your fitness goals as a single person is to do four things…

>Remove obstacles.
>Make it fun.
>Set goals.
>Reward yourself.

Here are some ways to stay motivated to get or keep fit:

- Make it social. Go to a regular class where you start to recognize the people, and maybe even make a gym friend or two. Having a social aspect to your workout makes it feel like less of a chore.

- Make a schedule. Treat working out like any other appointment, and stick with it! It's likely one of the most important appointments you'll have, because it ties directly to your health. I try to do mine in the morning. I find that it gives me incredible energy the rest of the day (counter-intuitive, I know), so I actually get *more* done on the days I exercise, not less.

- Enlist a friend or workout buddy. I started running last year. I hated running back then. I still do. So I enlisted a friend to run with me. When I say "enlisted" I mean bribed. (I think of it as strong encouragement. She thinks of it as extortion. PoTAYto – PoTAHto. Whatever. It worked. Moving on...) When our schedules mesh and we can run together, there's a 99% chance we'll actually run. When one of us can't make it, and we're left to run on our own, the chance of any sort of running happening plummets to about 20%. Just having that accountability, and the fear of looking like a flake or a slacker, is motivation enough for me.

- Take a dance or fitness class at a local community college. When you're paying for it, and being graded on it, there's a whole new level of motivation that doesn't exist when you're left to your own devices.

- Concentrate your workout. Find a workout DVD that specializes in shorter workouts that alternate between moderate activity and bursts of high-intensity activity. You don't need to spend hours at the gym. Many fitness experts say that 20-30 minutes a day is all you really need if you're a non-athlete who just wants to get healthier.

- Mix it up. One of the reasons I fail at working out is because I find the usual workouts mind-numbingly boring. Keep things interesting by changing up your routine. Do a dance class one day, go for a run the next, visit a yoga class, take a bike ride, hit the gym. An entire week can go by without repeating the same exercise. Having something new to look forward to each day removes some of the drudgery.

- Use a fitness tracker like MyFitnessPal or MapMyRun. These devices don't necessarily help me get through a workout, but they do inspire me to keep it up. I can look back on my progress and see how far I've come, and that's all the motivation I need to keep going.

- Dangle a carrot in front of yourself. Ok, I don't mean a *real* carrot – I mean a metaphorical one. Have your eye on a new outfit that you will buy when you lose that weight. Pick out a vacation destination as a reward for completing that marathon. Reward systems can be big motivators.

- Invest in a FitBit, Garmin, or other electronic reminder. These clever little electronic nags know when you've been inactive too long, and bug you mercilessly until you get up and get moving.

- Set attainable goals. If your goal is to lose weight, set a per-week goal – but make sure it's healthy and do-able. If you want to run a marathon, set mileage or time goals for your runs. Write them down (in ink) on a calendar or planner so you can see them every day. Having a specific goal, rather than a nebulous direction of "get healther," gives you something concrete to aim for.

- ϒ Set mini in-workout goals. When I started running, I would push myself by paying attention to when I wanted to give up. I would then look ahead to see what landmarks lay before me, and tell myself that I would run to that landmark, and then let myself walk. Once there, I would try to get to the next landmark, and so on. Eventually I would let myself walk for a few seconds, but creating those mini-goals really helped me step up my workout game.

- ϒ Turn everyday chores into your workout. We're all super busy these days – even us single folk. We don't have someone to vacuum or do the laundry for us while we're at the gym. So turn those tasks into your workout. As you're vacuuming, do lunges with every step. Wear wrist weights as you're folding laundry. Do leg lifts (side and back) while you're doing dishes. Be creative – there are dozens of ways to turn household chores into workouts.

- ϒ Use music to keep you going. Have you ever seen a movie before the background music has been added? I have, and let me tell you – it's usually snoozeville. There's a reason movies employ music as an emotional device. Music, like almost no other medium, has the power to make us feel. And feeling motivated is no exception. Make a personalized playlist of motivational music. Think "I Will Survive" or "Don't Stop Believin'" or whatever floats your motivational boat. Having those tunes as your personal soundtrack may just get you across that finish line. End scene.

- ⚑ Try an audio book. Many people, especially long-distance runners, swear by audio books. Even if you're a rockstar and run a 10-minute mile, it doesn't take too many miles before boredom sets in. Having an ongoing story to listen to can keep that boredom at bay.

- ⚑ Put on your workout clothes. For me, sometimes the hardest part of working out is getting started. I've found that if I just put on the clothes, I'm more likely to actually work out. I think to myself, "Well, I'm already dressed for it, I may as well do it." And before I know it, I've started working out. And then when I'm working out I think to myself, "Well, I've already started, I may as well finish." Just getting started can be the biggest hurdle you'll overcome.

- ⚑ Commit to your fitness plan publicly. We now live in the age of social media, where our every move is documented and shared. Use that modern-day voyeurism to your advantage. Set your goal publicly, then post your workouts, successes, and challenges. You may be amazed at how much support you get from the digital world. Not only does that inspire us to keep going, but it may also keep us accountable. And bonus: you'll probably get to post some really cool stuff.

🏋 Eat healthy. So far, all these points have focused on physical activity. But any chapter on fitness would be remiss if it didn't also include at least one bullet point on nutrition. It's said that 80% of your workout happens in the kitchen. That doesn't mean you do calisthenics in your kitchen (although you can, if you want). It simply means that 80% of your health is about what you eat. So here's where I restate what you already know.

- Stay away from processed and fast food.
- Eat whole foods.
- Focus on veggies and fruits
- Focus on lean proteins and good fats.
- Reduce sugar and bad carbs.

I hate to be so tiresome as to borrow an advertising slogan, but Nike really captured something when they said, "Just do it." That's both the easiest and hardest part of any fitness routine – just doing it. But ultimately, whether you're single or married, living alone or living with a crowd, you just have to do it.

So go get fit! Your body will thank you.

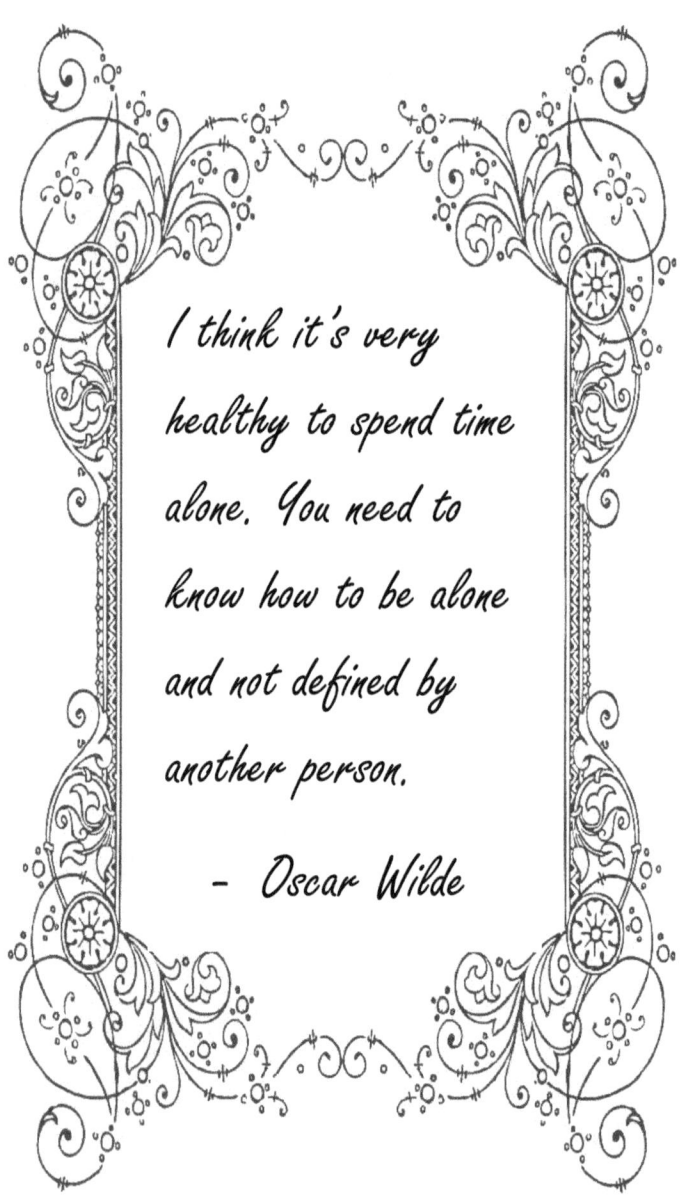

*I think it's very healthy to spend time alone. You need to know how to be alone and not defined by another person.*

*— Oscar Wilde*

# EMOTIONAL/MENTAL HEALTH

Every day we are bombarded with messages about how important it is to take care of our physical health. Whether it's news stories, or medical articles, or the latest fitness craze, we understand in no uncertain terms how important it is to take care of our bodies.

But what about our minds?

According to the National Institute of Health, there is a positive correlation between loneliness and the increased risk of mental health issues. Additionally, studies have shown that those who are chronically lonely suffer greater physical ailments and live shorter lives.

There are a lot of reasons why this tragic relationship exists, but I'll try to summarize it in an over-simplified, non-scientific explanation. Humans are social animals. Interacting in social groups is a fundamental need of our species. And when that need is not met, it negatively affects every other area of our lives.

And this presents a problem for us singles – especially as our friends start getting married and having families. When living alone we run the risk of getting too comfortable in our little fortress of solitude, and then we eventually eliminate the support structure of friends and family who meet our social needs and help us weather the bad times.

Obviously, the solution to this issue seems simple and straight-forward. Duh…hang out with friends more often. (See chapter 9.) But it's not that simple. It's a huge challenge to have meaningful hang-out time with friends when those friends have to juggle husbands/wives and babies and soccer games and puke and mountains of laundry and all the other things that come with marriage and family.

So, while the best and most effective solution would be to encourage and maintain meaningful, supportive relationships with friends, family, and significant others, this chapter will focus on exercising your mental health in between visits with friends and family by offering seven mental health exercises that don't rely 100% on other humans.

**Exercise 1: Daily Affirmations.**

Surround yourself with reminders of how awesome you are. I know that sounds a bit narcissistic. But in a world that still insists on judging a woman's worth by her marital status and whether or not she's had children, we need to remind ourselves how amazing we are. Affirmations aren't for women alone. Men living alone also need reminders that they are valuable. Without a significant other to tell us how pretty or smart or funny or whatever we are, we need to be our own cheerleaders. Tape a daily affirmation to your bathroom mirror so you see it (even if only subconsciously) every morning.

**Exercise 2: Surround Yourself with Positivity.**

Besides daily affirmations, there are a lot of other ways to create an environment of positivity.
- Frame pictures of family and friends that make you happy, and place them in areas you'll see every day.

- Place souvenirs from favorite trips or activities in prominent areas, so their memories will evoke feelings of happiness whenever you glimpse them.
- Keep yourself motivated and excited for your next dream, project, or adventure by creating a vision board. It could be of things you want to do or places you want to go, or even your next entrepreneurial business venture. Check out sites like Pinterest for ideas of things to include on your board. Hang it in the room where you spend the most time so you're guaranteed to see it every day.
- Indulge in your favorite color. Fill your home with throw pillows, cozy blankets, or accessories that showcase your favorite hue. Surrounding ourselves with things we love, even just a color, adds to our overall sense of well-being.
- Don't forget about your sense of smell. Smell has a surprising impact on our mood. Put some essential oil in a diffuser, or burn a soy or beeswax candle with a pleasing scent. Or, infuse your home with the scent of freshly baked cookies by...well, by baking cookies. Then share those goodies with a neighbor.

## Exercise 3: No One is a Rock, No One is an Island.

OK – you guessed it, I love Simon & Garfunkel. Have you ever listened to the lyrics of their song "I

Am a Rock?" The story is sad. Tragic. And way too familiar to a lot of us. If we have been wounded in the past, it is tempting, and often seems easier, to shut ourselves off from people – to isolate ourselves and build walls around our hearts so we don't have to suffer the pain of being hurt again. And while it may feel safer to turn ourselves into a metaphorical rock or an untouchable island, the reality is that a rock does feel pain and an island often cries.

Make an effort to open your doors (the literal doors of your home, and the metaphorical doors of your heart) and let people in. Share your space, share yourself, and embrace the love that inevitably will come pouring in. Start small by just inviting a few friends over for dinner, or a movie, or game night. It can be a very simple, no-stress evening of yoga pants and potluck. As you get more comfortable hosting, increase the number of guests and vary the theme. Eventually, being open to friendship and love will feel normal again, and a lot less scary.

## Exercise 4: Keep Your Mental Palette Varied and Balanced.

Have you ever noticed how our mood changes with every book we read or movie we watch? Funny TV makes me laugh out loud. Swashbuckling novels make me want to take fencing lessons. And girl-power films make me feel like I can conquer the world.

It's important to recognize the impact entertainment media has on our mood and mental health, and be mindful of what we're feeding our brains. Don't binge on all sad movies, scary books, or fluffy TV. Mix it up with documentaries, dramas, comedies, and yes – even those beloved rom-coms (my personal favorites). Just like a balanced diet of food helps keep the body healthy, a balanced diet of entertainment helps keep our mind healthy.

**Exercise 5: Get a Pet.**

There are countless research studies that show a positive correlation between pet ownership and improved mental health. If you're the kind of person who likes statistics and medical jargon, I'll let you look up those studies on the Google machine. But for the purposes of this chapter, I'll summarize the highlights.

But first I feel I need to restate what seems like an obvious warning. DO NOT get a pet just as a mental health aid. Pets should be part of your family. They require, and deserve, love and attention and exercise and a special place in your heart and home. If you do not, or cannot, give them these things, bypass this exercise and move on to the next.

▸ Caring for a pet gets us out of ourselves and

forces us to focus on taking care of another living being.
- Dogs help their owners get more exercise. Dogs require walks – several of them per day. They also benefit from training and trips to the dog park, all of which also give their owners a little much-needed exercise, too. This is especially helpful for people battling depression.
- Cat owners should not feel left out. A 2011 survey reported that a whopping 87% of people surveyed who owned a cat experienced a positive impact on their sense of well-being, and 76% felt that having a cat companion helped them cope with their day-to-day life. Petting a cat has also been reported to have soothing effects on humans, which lowers blood pressure and reduces stress hormones. (This is true of petting dogs, too.)
- Pets help us feel not so lonely. Having another life force in our presence, even one of another species, gives us someone to share our life and space with. And pets are funny! They have unique personalities all their own, and have a way of making us laugh at their antics. And, at the risk of exposing myself as a crazy cat/dog lady, they also give us something to talk to and interact with.
- Dogs can introduce us to more humans. Dog owners take their four-legged companions on walks and to the dog park, which often leads to meeting other dog owners and establishing

friendships.
- The benefits of pet ownership are not limited to dogs and cats. Reports show that owning, interacting, and caring for almost any living thing, including rabbits, horses, guinea pigs, and even fish, help to reduce stress and anxiety, and improve mental and physical health.

**Exercise 6: Keep Your World Big.**

It is easy to get trapped in our own little sphere of existence. We are so caught up in the everyday life of being us that we forget there is a great big world out there – especially when there's no one encouraging us to go and see and do and experience new things. It is up to us to expand our world, so here are some ways to do that.

- Read a diverse selection of books, including informational, biographical, fiction, non-fiction, and cultural.
- Watch a varied line-up of movies and TV, including dramas, comedies, romances, cultural, documentaries, and travel.
- Engage in the world around you by joining groups and organizations that speak to you, like volunteer organizations, environmental groups, recreation clubs, and hobbyists.
- Watch the news or read the paper to keep tabs on local, national, and world events. Don't limit your

viewing to just conservative or liberal programming. Watch a cross-section of available offerings, including foreign news outlets (which I find offer the most objective views of what's happening in our own backyard).
- Be a part of your community by attending (or better yet, volunteering) for local events and activities.

**Exercise 7: Be Kind to Your Mental Health.**

Give your mental health a little bit of the same love, caring, and attention you give your body. Think about the things our bodies need to survive. Bodies need:

- To be fed
- To rest
- To work out
- To get help if something goes wrong

So it makes sense to maintain your brain the same way you maintain your body.

- Feeding your brain includes both what information you put into your brain and what nourishment you put into your body.
    - As a single person, it is very easy to opt for fast food or processed packaged foods. Unfortunately, there is a strong correlation between processed foods, particularly

processed meats, and mental health issues – especially as we age. So cut back on the convenience stuff. Instead opt for whole foods, and focus on foods that boost brain function, such as healthy fats (fish, olive oil, avocados), dark leafy greens, and nuts. A quick online search will yield comprehensive lists of what to eat and what to avoid to maintain brain health. It won't be easy to give up those delicious but unhealthy foods, but your brain will thank you.

- Seek to fill your brain with healthy and substantive information from a variety of sources, (see exercise #6).

▸ Your brain needs to rest and recharge the same as your body does. There are plenty of studies that link insufficient sleep with mental health issues, such as depression, anxiety, and Alzheimer's disease. This, I'm happy to say, may be one of the few things that's actually easier if you live alone. Without a spouse, children, or roommate to keep us up, we have more control over our sleep habits. So make it a priority to get the recommended amount of quality sleep for your age.

▸ Exercise your brain! We've all heard the warnings

about sedentary lifestyles and what they do to our bodies. But a sedentary mental lifestyle is just as harmful to our brains. Give your brain a good workout by playing games, learning a new skill, taking up a hobby, or practicing a foreign language. The more you work out your brain, the better your long term brain function.

- When we live alone, we don't have another person to alert us if something seems off in our mood or behavior. Consequently, mental health issues can creep up without us realizing what's happening. We must make a conscious effort to pay attention to what our minds are telling us, and if something feels off, visit a professional for a little mental health check-in.

Your brain is no different than your knee or intestines as far as its need for occasional medical attention. And while it's perfectly acceptable to see a doctor if something feels off in your knee or gut, sadly, there is still a stigma that exists around needing a little mental health help. But that stigma is slowly fading, and people are being educated about the need for good mental health support. That brain boost can take many forms. It doesn't always mean intense soul-wrenching couch sessions where you leave feeling emotionally shredded. Sometimes it's as simple as using an online resource or app, like *Headspace* or

*Stop, Breathe & Think.* Maybe it's joining a support group – a group of people who have gone through, or are going through, the same challenges you're facing. Or perhaps you'd benefit from weekly check-ins with a mentor or life coach. It could be some one-on-one time with a church or guidance counselor, or even a more traditional approach with a therapist or psychologist/psychiatrist.

Getting mental health assistance is not a sign of weakness – it demonstrates you are strong enough and smart enough to seek a little help when you need it.

Living alone comes with a whole lot of mental and emotional freedom. But it's not always a stroll down easy street. Sometimes it is more of a challenge to maintain good emotional and mental health when living alone, so singletons must be incredibly self-aware and proactive with preventative care.

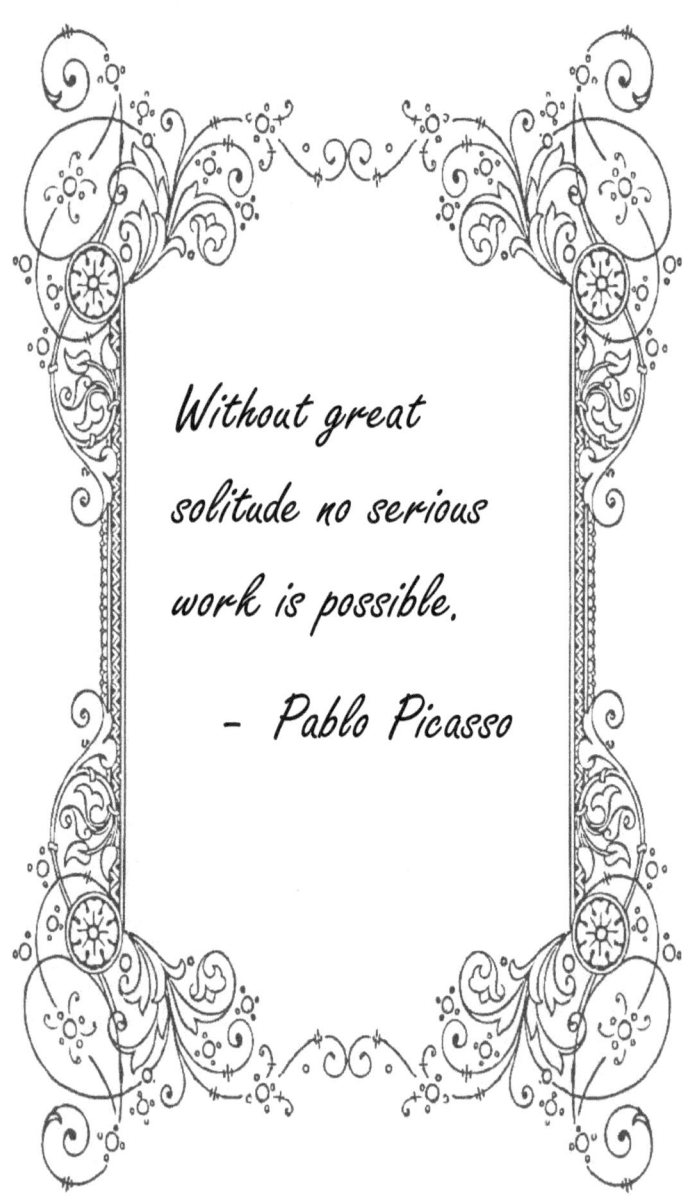

*Without great solitude no serious work is possible.*

*— Pablo Picasso*

# FINANCES

There are so many wonderful, freeing, empowering aspects that come with living alone. Many of which I've written about in earlier chapters of this book. But not all is rosy in the singles universe (as I've also written about within these pages). But when you're single and living alone, dealing with the financials can feel like walking a precarious tightrope with no safety net and certain doom lurking just one wrong step away.

When I say "dealing with the financials," I don't mean just the physical act of paying the bills each month. With electronic bill-pay options, and automated electronic transfers, the act of paying bills is easier than ever. What I mean is making sure you have enough money coming in each month to meet all the bills that need to go out.

If you're married, living with a significant other, or have a roommate, you likely have the benefit of two incomes and shared expenses to lighten your financial load. But people living alone don't have such luxury. For those of us baching it (can a girl say "baching it?" Well, I just did, so there it is), we must bear the entire financial burden on our slender shoulders. And to add an extra layer of challenges, researchers have shown that the substantial additional stress of having to handle everything alone, and not having the financial help (or emotional support) of a partner, cause solo dwellers to fall toward the bottom of the wellness scale when it comes to finances.

There are ways to overcome these challenges. And one of the ways to reduce the biggest stressor of our singles lives is to make sure we are financially comfortable. I don't mean wealthy (although that would be nice, too). I mean putting yourself in a position that you are living comfortably within your means, and that you have your own financial safety net should you encounter a hurdle.

Here are some ways to start that process.

$    Ensure your spending is in line with your income. Track your spending for a month or two to find out exactly where your money is going. You might be surprised to find you're not spending nearly as much at Starbucks as you feared, or that you have a shoe or power tool addiction. This is an important step, because you cannot plan how to get where you want to go unless you know where you are now.

$ Create a budget. Remember, your budget should be constructed from your net income, not your gross income. Your gross income is what you make at work. Your net income is what you get to take home after taxes and other deductions. Your net income can be as much as 30% or more less than your gross income, which is gross! (See what I did there? Gross vs. gross? It's a homonym – two words that are spelled the same but mean....aw, never mind.) On the next page is a very general list of percentages to shoot for, and space to write in your totals.

Of course, every person is different, so your percentages might vary from these. If you tithe 10% to your church or religious organization, you must make room for that in your budget, which means reducing 10% from another category. If you have higher debt or housing costs, you'll need to adjust accordingly. If you must also pay for childcare or pet care, that will be a huge adjustment to these figures. But this is a very general worksheet to get you started with your own monthly budget.

| My Monthly Net Pay = $ | | |
|---|---|---|
| **Expense Description** | **Percentage** | **$ per month** |
| **Fixed Expenses** | | |
| Housing | 25-30% | |
| Utilities (inc. phone and web) | 10-15% | |
| Insurances | 10-15% | |
| Debt Repayment | 10% | |
| | | |
| **Variable Expenses** | | |
| Food | 10-15% | |
| Transportation | 10-15% | |
| Savings | 10% | |
| Recreation/Entertainment | 5-10% | |
| Clothing/Shoes | 5% | |
| Charity/Misc. | 5% | |
| | | |
| **Totals** | 100% | |

$ Build your emergency savings fund. Pay yourself as if you were your most important bill. Putting 10% into savings is the standard. But if you can do more, or put the extra into other investments, that's better. Since we don't have a second income to act as our financial safety net to get us through tough times, we are our own safety net and we absolutely must have this account. Plan for an emergency fund of at least six months' worth of expenses. The standard used to be three months' worth of savings – but in today's tough job economy, that figure has been bumped to six months. It is important to note that this emergency account is not the same as a general savings account. This is not the place to dip into for vacations, cars, clothes, power tools, or even those really awesome Prada shoes you cannot live without. This account should be completely separate from your other accounts, so it's not easy to access, and should be strictly reserved for living emergencies (job loss, etc.) only. Once that emergency account is fully funded, start funneling money into your investments or retirement funds.

$ Utilize money-saving and bill-pay apps and websites. There are a gazillion apps and websites to choose from to help you pay down debt and increase savings. You'll want to do a little research of your own, since new and better apps come on the market every day. But as of the writing of this book, here are a few of my favorites: Mint, Shoeboxed, Acorns, Qoins.

$ Save on taxes. Most singles file their taxes as "single." And most do not own their own homes, which means they have far fewer tax breaks than their friends who are married, have children, or own homes. If you're in the income bracket where taxes are an issue, consider contributing to a retirement fund that will reduce your tax burden. There are many avenues to explore, so talk to a financial adviser or tax expert to find the strategy right for you. And bonus: in addition to reducing your taxes, you'll contribute to your retirement years, which is another area where singles struggle.

$ Learn to cook. And, more importantly, learn to *like* to cook. According to the Harvard Business Review, only 10% of Americans like to cook. 90% either hate to cook or are on the fence. Cooking for one is not always fun, (which is why I have entire chapters on cooking and grocery shopping in this book), and dining out is oh-so easy and tempting. But let's look at dining out strictly from a financial point of view. If an average meal costs $10 (which is actually a bit of an underestimate), and a single person goes out to lunch three times a week, and to dinner twice a week, that's $50/week or $200/month in take-out food. Yikes! If you are trying to reduce your monthly budget, have tracked your expenditures (as suggested in the first bullet of this list), and spend more than $100 a month on restaurant or take-out food, you may want to start looking for recipes instead of menus. Limiting your dining out budget to $25/week may feel impossible. But convenience and restaurant food adds up quickly, and it's one of the easiest ways to start to get a budget under control.

$ Cut the cord. Gone are the days where a landline is necessary. The trend is toward "cord cutting," meaning that home phones are being replaced by mobile phones. Considering that a landline can cost $50-$100 a month, depending on your provider, cutting the cord can lead to significant savings! As always, you must decide if this is the right choice for you. If you live in an area where cell service is sketchy or non-existent, you'll want to keep a landline for safety reasons.

$ Consider a smart TV over cable or satellite service. I recently purchased a Roku smart TV. Before buying it, I didn't realize how much it would change my TV viewing habits. There are so many streaming services available through your smart devices that cable and satellite services are becoming obsolete. And with a-la-cart channel providers on the rise, it is becoming less and less necessary to subscribe to a television provider.

$ Research disability insurance and long-term care coverage. Of course we hope the worst will never happen, but it might be worth your peace-of-mind to invest in coverage, just in case. Without a second income to fall back on, singles have extra motivation to include this type of coverage in their insurance portfolio. A word of warning: it is pricey. But if the worst happens, you may find it's worth it.

$ Consider living in a smaller space. Most people think they need more living space than they actually do. Look to the European and Asian cultures for inspiration. Their homes average 50% smaller than homes in the United States – not because of a lack of wealth or income, but mostly because of culture. In the U.S. we love our "stuff," and we need space to keep it. Living in a smaller space means you have to buy less stuff to fill it. Having a smaller space to heat or cool means spending less money on heating and air conditioning costs. Additionally, incidental costs such as cleaning supplies, food, etc., are less than they would be in a larger space. There are a lot of creative ways to use smaller spaces – check out small-space or tiny house websites for ideas. Invest in multitasking furniture pieces and kitchen gadgets (such as a coffee table that doubles as storage or a multi-cooker appliance) to double the usage of your stuff, thereby requiring less square footage.

$ Rethink need vs want. Much of the stuff we think we need, is actually stuff that we just really, really want. We want it so much that it feels like a need. Sure it is fun to have new shoes. As a self-proclaimed shoe addict it pains me to say it, but I really do not need as many shoes as I think I do. So having an honest conversation with yourself about what you truly need can end up saving a ton of money. Additionally, lightening the load of "stuff" can create a freeing feeling, and cost less in moving or storage expenses.

$ Consider a side hustle to make extra cash. Evaluate your talents – are you a good writer, artist, upcycle guru, or something else? Tap into your hidden skills to make some extra cash. Whether you sell stuff on Etsy, take copywriting jobs, drive for Uber or Lyft, or sell your art at craft fairs, side jobs can bring in extra income that can then go to paying off debt or having a little fun. I once turned my thrift store and yard sale habit into a business by reselling curated items at an antique market. It gave me justification for my habit, and contributed to my travel fund, which ultimately took me on a dream vacation to Ireland.

$ Designate a "just in case" ally. Have your usernames and passwords, plus a general list of all the bills you pay monthly, and other important info (relatives names/numbers, insurance info, etc.) listed in a safe place. Then ask a trusted friend or family member to be your helper in case you are too sick or injured to take care of business. Make sure you take care of these details and tell them the secret location of your list while you are healthy. You may even want to give them a key to your place. If something very bad happens, and you're unable to communicate, it may take a legal battle to gain access to this info, so make sure it's all taken care of before anything happens. Hopefully you'll never need to put that friend to work, but it will be a relief to know it's taken care of, just in case.

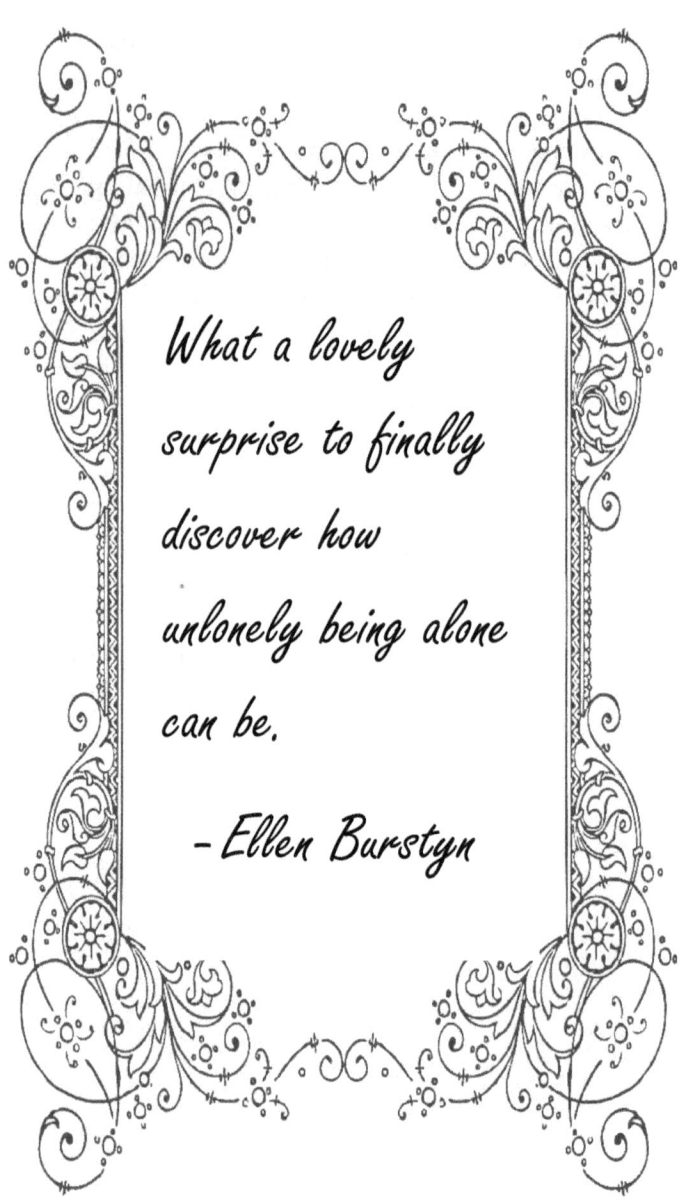

What a lovely surprise to finally discover how unlonely being alone can be.

– Ellen Burstyn

# SURVIVING THE HOLIDAYS

Ahhhh...the holidays. It's the most wonderful time of the year. Right?

Not always. Especially if you're single and live alone.

Holidays are notoriously geared for family, significant others, and children. So if you don't have those, it is very easy to feel left out and alone. Depression is a common occurrence during these most festive times. So how do you combine living alone and the holidays without falling into the pit of despair? That is the big question.

One of my favorite tactics is to decorate. Sure, I may be the only one to see the decorations, but why shouldn't I get the joy of holiday decor just because I live alone? I want all the cheer of Christmas, the elegance of New Year's Eve, and the patriotism of the 4$^{th}$ of July just as much as those who share their domiciles with loved ones.

My friend Malinda, who also produces my web series, is newly single. After spending many years single, and then married, and then single again, she has had experience surviving the holidays from both sides of the married fence. It's not easy to spend holidays alone and maintain a positive outlook, so I asked her to write about her survival tactics in an article for our website asinglegirlsguideto.com. With her permission, I have reprinted that article below. Immediately following her article, I have added a special addendum dedicated to the king (or queen?) of coupledom holidays, Valentine's Day.

### *Suddenly Single for the Holidays*

*On my wedding day, I thought the single life was over. Never again would I be dateless or scrambling to make plans for significant occasions.*

*Then, one Halloween, my marriage imploded and I was suddenly dramatically single just in time for the holidays.*

*Joy.*

*Not only can traditional holiday celebrations be awkward when you're flying solo, but I had additional emotional trauma to keep me company. Yet, during one of the most difficult seasons of my life, a little holiday festivity crept in among the awkward gatherings and my personal pity parties. Believe it or not, I learned a few things that might make solo holidays a little cheerier.*

### Kick the "shoulds" to the curb.

*Expectations based on past holidays and Norman Rockwell paintings will merely inspire disappointment. Spend your daydreaming on creating a fresh vision for your holidays.*

### Decide what really matters and what the holidays mean to you.

*Is Christmas a celebration of faith? If so, choose activities and traditions that focus on those beliefs. Is Thanksgiving about gratitude? What can you do to really concentrate your thankfulness? Get to the heart of the matter – because the reason for the season is not relationship status (let's just pretend Valentine's Day isn't a thing right now, k?).*

***Create new traditions.***

*Keep the stuff you love, if you can, of course. We all love some good warm-'n'-fuzzy nostalgia. But it's a new year! All traditions had a first time, so what can you create now that will last for years to come? Whether on your own or shared with a loved one, here's your chance to write some really good stories for future holidays.*

***To be or not to be – alone that is.***

*Many times it helps to avoid excessive alone time. But if that's your thing, be purposeful about it. Those cliché bubble baths with wine and a good book are popular for a reason. Constructive alone time is very different than the usual "Well, Netflix, it looks like it's just you and me. Again." However, when alone time just leads your mind down a trail of holiday sorrow, it's time to gather whatever energy you've got and make some plans with a friend or family member. And when schedules aren't cooperative, you've now got a great opportunity to do some gift shopping or craft-making. Even if you're not in their company, thinking about people you love and focusing your time and energy doing something kind for them is a great alternative.*

**Give.**

*Spreading love and joy to others is good for the soul, and a great way to celebrate. Money is fast and easy, but an investment of time in a cause goes a long way. Plus, plugging into your community is about as far from being alone as it gets.*

**You've heard it over and over again, but self-care is actually important.**

*Oh, this is a whole article subject in itself. We're so good at neglecting our own needs, even when we're so miserable we can't get out of our own heads. You know the downward spiral, and it's oddly tempting just to curl up in the sadness even though it makes us feel worse. Let's analyze all of that later. In the meantime, make sure to take care of yourself, even if you don't feel like it. Yes, that means reasonably healthy food choices, plenty of rest, some exercise, and all that stuff you know you need to do. These small details make a big difference and are the foundation for surviving the most, um, wonderful time of the year.*

***Take the opportunity to learn, explore, and change.***

*It's easy to reflect on past holidays and feel wistful and bittersweet. Honor the good memories, while creating new ones. Discover something about yourself, your family history, or your neighborhood that you never knew before. Try a new skill or hobby. Be adventurous and make a new friend or two. Take a mini road trip and do your holiday prep in a nearby town – a change of scenery can be surprisingly inspirational.*

***Holiday travel is popular for a reason.***

*If you're up for the adventure of crowded airports and navigating good deals, why not treat yourself to an adventure-for-one (or one with a few pals)? Maybe a snow lodge skiing weekend with a cozy fireside? Or skip the winter blues in favor of a tropical yuletide?*

*Ring in the New Year with style in the big city? Discover other cultures' Christmas traditions? There's a whole planet of possibility.*

*Life throws us into places we don't want to be. So, why stay there longer than necessary? The only way to heal is to get up and try to move forward...even if that forward movement starts as a crawl. Forget the boring "ideal" notions of the season and create your own happy holiday. Being alone for the holidays doesn't have to mean being lonely.*

Alright, as promised, here's an attempt to turn the dreaded Valentine's Day into something you look forward to...

**Valentine's Day (aka Singles Awareness Day)**

As a young girl I loved Valentine's Day. My sixth-grade self would get all twitterpated thinking about dropping that old-school valentine's card onto the desk of the boy I had a crush on. I would spend hours poring over my pack of Peanuts or Strawberry Shortcake or Scooby Doo cards to find just the right one that contained the subtext I was trying to convey – convinced that my secret crush would read between the lines and understand my feelings for him. I was well aware it was only a school-girl crush, but I dreamed of the day the feelings I had for my sixth-grade Romeo would translate to a real adult romance. (What I didn't know then, that I do now, is that boys are never good at reading subtext, whether they're 10 or 40.)

As an adult, I have yet to experience the kind of Valentine's Day I envisioned in my school-girl dreams. But I have not given up hope that it might still happen. In the meantime, I have perfected many fail-safe tactics to navigate what many call Singles Awareness Day (or S.A.D. for short). Instead of lamenting the fact that I usually spend this Hallmark holiday without a handsome man by my side, I use it to celebrate the amazing life I have created for myself. In short, I am my own valentine. Malinda, who wrote the previous holiday section, is recently single. So we compared notes and came up with this list of 20 strategies to enjoy this Valentine's Day, not dread it. (Full disclosure – most of these ideas are Malinda's. She's amazing that way.)

So, instead of attempting to burn down the Valentine aisle at the local Walmart, why not try one of these activities, guaranteed to make you feel glad, not S.A.D.

***Warning***: Since the negative effects of Valentine's Day tend to hit women more than men, you'll notice this section has a very definite female slant. I apologize in advance to all the male readers. But even if you are of the male persuasion, you may still be able to use some of these tips. So read on, my masculine friend! Read on...

- ♥ Host a Galentine's party. Fans of *Parks and Recreation* will know what that is. (If you're unsure, check out the episode clips online – they'll explain everything.) Essentially, it's a day for girls to celebrate friends. Traditionally (can something so new be called a tradition?) it's held on February 13. But I contend that it can be held any day.

- ♥ Pamper yourself with a mani/pedi or a day at the spa. This could be pricey, depending on where you go – but an investment in ourselves is always worth it.

- ♥ If finding a relationship is a high priority for you, use the day to make a plan of action. Research dating websites to find one that fits you and write a compelling profile. Find clubs and organizations for things about which you are passionate (hiking? animal rescue? beach clean-up? etc.), and join them. Many relationships start with a shared activity. And if you don't find your Mr. or Mrs. Right, it is likely you'll make some cool new friends – and that is always a good thing.

- ♥ Do a little research on St. Valentine. Yes, he was a real guy, and did some cool stuff.

- ♥ Go old school and send your friends fun valentines… either the cute kid ones or bust out the construction paper and glitter and make your own.

- ♥ Read Jane Austen, or another satirical romance writer who pokes fun at the male/female dynamic, and the inevitable ridiculousness that is inherent in any relationship – regardless of the century. If you're not a reader, consider renting a movie. There are a lot of great films based on classic novels, and well worth the time and investment.

- ♥ Bake! Then share with friends, family, and neighbors. Nothing says "I care about you" quite like a plate of peanut butter chocolate chip cookies.

- ♥ Treat yourself to a very nice bottle of wine, and some high-end chocolate. Hey – the news is full of reports about the health benefits of wine and dark chocolate, so consider this a win-win.

♥ Write a love letter – a sincere note to someone you care about that is so thoughtful it will make them cry.

♥ Design a valentine themed act of kindness, and then do it on the 14th. It could be donating to a women's shelter, or picking up the tab of the person behind you in the Starbucks drive-thru, or anything else you can think of.

♥ Surprise anyone you encounter on the 14th with a valentine treat of some sort. (Hint: save the home-baked goodies for people you know. For strangers, try something non-edible or store-bought. Dollar stores are great places to find these treasures.)

♥ Send a valentine package to a kid in your life, even if they live just down the street. Sparkly heart stickers or a new book are an awesome surprise for a kid – plus it's great to get fun mail and it makes a kid feel special.

♥ Buy yourself fresh flowers. Having fresh flowers is cheerful, brightens any room, and they smell amazing.

- If you want to avoid S.A.D., turn on loud music and clean the house. Channel the inner valentine rage, then feel great when your house is clean.

- Leave the country to avoid the nonsense. Not all countries are as Valentine's Day obsessed as the U.S. In some countries, February 14 is just February 14.

- Deliver valentines to a nursing home, or find out if you can take craft supplies and make them with residents.

- Read a valentine themed book to kids at the library. (This one takes advanced prep, because you have to sign up and sometimes be interviewed.)

- Show love to the earth… pick up litter, recycle, make valentine-y canvas bags, be an activist for an environmental cause, etc.

- Show love to people in need and donate to your favorite charity with a valentine note.

- Indulge in a bubble bath, a good book, some candles, and a pizza. Because when you're alone on Valentine's Day, it doesn't matter if you have garlic breath.

♥ Bonus: Partner with a veteran's organization and send old-school valentine cards to military members serving overseas. This has to be done weeks in advance in order for them to arrive on time, but you get the warm-fuzzy feeling of knowing that someone thousands of miles from home is reading your card and probably smiling.

Here's the deal: even if we live alone and don't have a significant other in our lives, most of us are surrounded by more love than we realize. Friends, family, and even pets, are a tremendous source of unconditional love. So use the holidays to celebrate that love and share it with others. There can never be too much love in this world.

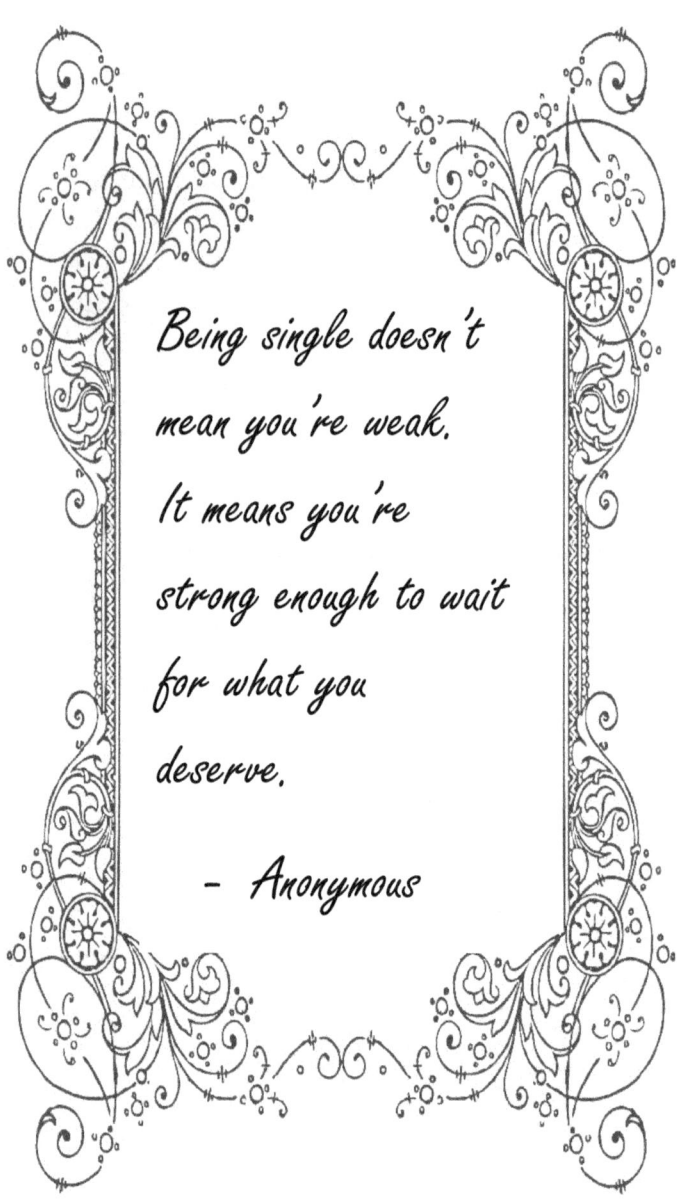

*Being single doesn't mean you're weak. It means you're strong enough to wait for what you deserve.*

*— Anonymous*

# SOMETIMES IT'S NO FUN

So far, this book has focused on the positive aspects of living alone. Or, how to take a challenging aspect of solo living and turn it into a positive. It's empowering. It's freeing. It's fun. Well, usually it's fun. But here's the time where I have to interject a little dose of harsh reality.

Sometimes it's no fun.

I just moved. "Moved" doesn't seem to fully describe

the overwhelming, time-consuming, all-encompassing events of the last few months. In the last few months I have renovated my old house, sold that house, moved everything into a storage unit, traveled to New Zealand, traveled to Arizona, traveled to Washington D.C., traveled to San Francisco, purchased a new house, renovated the new house, moved everything from the storage unit into the new house, and for the last two weeks have been existing in what has felt like a mountain range of moving boxes and furniture obstacles – all while continuing to maintain a career.

And most of that was done completely alone. Alone. Solo. Unaccompanied. Companionless. You get the idea.

I often write about the joys of being single. The freedom of not having to plan my life around another person's schedule. The empowerment of taking charge of your own life. The encouragement to start living a full life now instead of waiting for Prince(ess) Charming to show up first.

And all of that still holds true. But that's not the entire story.

I don't often write about the sleepless nights worrying about money. In Southern California, as in other parts of the country, it's nearly impossible to live on a single income.

I don't often write about the panic-inducing reality of facing major tasks alone. My latest major task was unpacking. Facing a Mt. Everest of moving boxes alone made tears appear in my eyes without warning. It was daunting. It seemed like an unending and insurmountable task. (Fortunately, my mom spent a few days with me and helped me tame the mountains of boxes.)

I don't often write about the major hiccups in an otherwise good plan. A few weeks after moving in, a day of heavy water usage caused a huge plumbing issue to rear its smelly head. I won't go into details, but if you imagine an outhouse overflowing into your sinks, you'll get the picture.

I don't often write about the drudgery of doing everyday tasks alone. There's no one to do the grocery shopping while I finish laundry. There's no one to do the dishes or cooking while I run to the pharmacy. There's no one to take care of the pets if I have to travel.

It's just me, and me alone.

Yes – I do have friends and family who would be willing to help if I asked. But all of them have busy lives of their own, and I feel bad, not to mention a bit pathetic, taking them away from their busy lives to help me. No – this is the path I chose and I must find a way to work through it. Sure – I could have married the wrong man just so I didn't have to face the world alone. I could have married a good friend just so I didn't have to deal with disgusting plumbing issues myself. But I didn't. I chose to remain single until the right man appeared in my life. And to date, Mr. Charming hasn't yet appeared on my doorstep. And I'm OK with that. I'm thrilled with my single life.

But once in a while I'm reminded how much easier things might be if I had someone with whom to share the burden. I'm not saying a single person isn't capable of doing all of this on his or her own. We are. And I am. I'm just saying that as much as I love my life, I have to be honest and say that sometimes it would be nice to have that special someone by my side to help me do the heavy lifting. Sometimes the weight of the world is a lot to bear alone.

So this is the reality-check chapter. Be prepared to have down days. They will happen. There will be days you just want to throw your hands in the air and wave your white flag of surrender. And that's OK. Let yourself experience them. Get frustrated. Get angry. Cry, if you feel like it. Living alone has a lot of advantages, and a whole lot of perks. But it also has its distinct disadvantages. And if you're living the solo life for now, you must expect that you will eventually experience them. You will have to accept that sometimes you will be lonely. But the truth is, very often married people are lonely too.

Preparation will help you through these dark hours. Prepare a survival kit. It might be an inspirational book and some gourmet chocolates. Maybe it's a pact with friends to get you out of the house when you start to feel this way. Or, perhaps it's delving into a Bible study or other study of faith. The goal is to let yourself experience the downtimes while providing a path to climb out of the darkness. Because as wonderful as it is, sometimes it's no fun being single alone.

The thing to remember, even in the darkest hours, is that tough times will eventually pass. Hang in there, keep up the good fight, and things will get better. The proverbial sun will eventually rise, its warm light will chase away the darkness, and you will be able to see all the joys of being single and living alone once again.

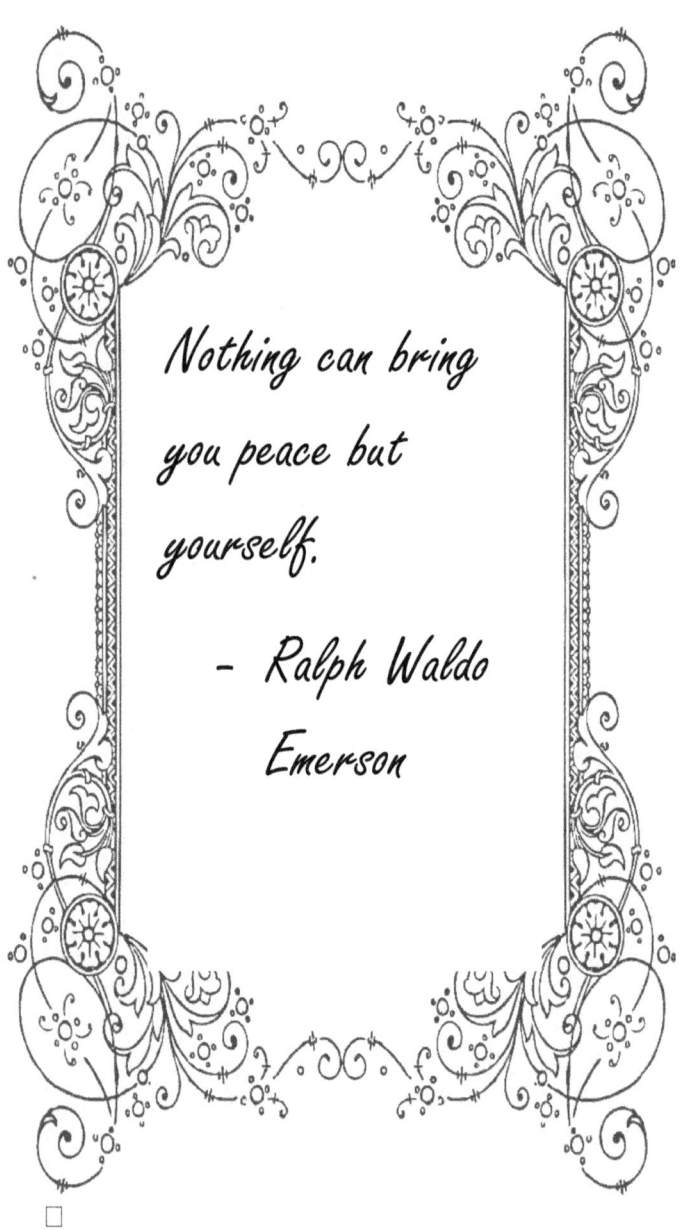

*Nothing can bring you peace but yourself.*

*— Ralph Waldo Emerson*

# 15

# STAYING MOTIVATED

An unexpected challenge of living alone is staying motivated. It doesn't seem like it would be a big deal. After all, life has the same basic requirements, whether you live alone or with a tribe. But I think most people underestimate the motivating power of people who share your living space.

Married people, people with kids, or even those with roommates have built-in motivators. Kids have a funny habit of needing food, clean clothes, and to get to school, so parents have no choice but to get off their keesters and get stuff done. Spouses or significant others can be drivers for activities, and can encourage their partners in their extra-curricular endeavors. Roommates can also be friends who motivate you to clean the house, or better yet, get out of it.

But those who live alone have no such external motivators. We have to summon the motivation from within, even when there's no pressing reason to do so. Dishes? They can wait until tomorrow, or the next day, or the next – no one's going to notice anyway. Shave my legs? I'm not dating anyone right now, and it's winter, so no one's going to care. Leave the house? Most of my friends have spouse/kid commitments and can't come out to play. So I can go out to dinner and a movie alone. Again. No thank you.

There's a lot to be said for the freedom and uncomplicated nature of living alone. But here's the thing…I work better in a collaborative environment than I do in isolation. Bouncing ideas off other people, being inspired by their ideas, and letting energy fuel each other is where some of my best work happens. My creativity is sparked and my motivation set on fire when I can share projects, goals, and aspirations with other people. I am a self-starter in many respects, and can have the determination of steel when I set my mind on something.

But manufacturing motivation takes a lot more energy than harnessing the naturally-occurring motivation that is generated by engaging with other people. Consequently, living alone presents a unique set of challenges. Sometimes even the simplest, most mundane things seem beyond my ability to tackle. I occasionally find myself staring at my walls wondering what to do with myself, but not feeling motivated to do much of anything. Time is then hungrily gobbled up by my latest social media or content streaming obsession. Time is one of our most valuable assets, and it feels like a crime to waste it. We'll never get it back, so we have to make sure that every minute of time is exchanged for something equal to its worth.

Here are some ways I stay motivated. I pray they help you not waste a single precious moment of this amazing life.

- 🕐 Figure out your intrinsic motivators, and then fill your life with them. Intrinsic motivators are those things we feel passionately about. They are the things that would get us out of bed every day and we'd do for free, if we were independently wealthy and didn't have to work for a living. Focusing on the things that make our souls sing creates its own motivation. Is it music? Nature? Crafting? Animals? Children? The arts? Writing?

Woodworking? Something else? And bonus: figuring out what our intrinsic motivators are might lead us into new career paths and introduce us to amazing new people.

🕒 Based on your intrinsic motivators, make a list of all the things you want to do...and then set out a plan to do them. Does volunteering make you feel lighter than air? Have you always wanted to write the next great American novel? Do you harbor an inner desire to learn to tap dance? Make a list, and then make a plan. But don't make a "someday" plan. Make a plan with concrete dates and appointments. Book a class. Schedule a lesson. Join a club that holds regular meetings. Make a promise to a friend. "Someday" lists rarely get done. But I find that if I book something – especially if it's something I paid for – I am far less likely to flake. And bonus: once you take the first step, subsequent steps feel easier.

🕒 Enlist a friend. Friends can not only keep us accountable for doing what we say we're going to do, but can also be that source of external motivation singles might be missing. For example – I adore dancing, and would happily take dance class after dance class after dance class until I dropped from sheer exhaustion. However, even though I know it's important and a necessary part of life, I loathe, hate, despise exercise for the sake of exercise. I find the gym mind-numbingly boring, and until recently the only time you'd find me running is if a T-Rex was chasing me. But, I absolutely love doing these things if I'm doing them with a friend. Sharing experiences with a friend turns a solo endeavor into a shared experience, and the motivation naturally flows. And bonus: both you AND your friend benefit from the deal.

- Set standards and schedules for yourself and your house – and stick to them. I have a "10 minutes to company" standard when it comes to my house. That means I keep my house clean enough that it can be ready to entertain guests with just 10 minutes' notice. I also have a schedule for cleaning. Dishes are dealt with before going to bed every night. Bedding is laundered every Saturday morning. You get the idea. Of course, the schedule is flexible and often changes to accommodate my busy life. But I do not allow myself to deviate much, because in the realm of living alone it is very easy to become lazy and let things go. So, unless cleaning is one of your intrinsic motivators, treat it like part of your job. Schedule cleaning like you'd schedule a meeting, and then revel in the sense of accomplishment once it's done. And bonus: studies have shown that keeping your house clean and organized increases happiness and decreases stress. Win-win!

🕐 Find a local hangout. As tempting as it is to play the Miss Havisham role and become an eccentric recluse, isolation is not healthy. So besides work and home, find a third place to cool your jets. Maybe it's the gym. (Hahaha – no.) Maybe it's the neighborhood Starbucks or local library. (Ooh – they should put a Starbucks inside the library! What a great idea! Sometimes I'm a legit genius.) Just getting out of my normal surroundings, and being around the energy of others inspires me to get moving on my long overdue list of "somedays." And bonus: finding a hangout that speaks to your sensibilities will put you in a position to meet other people like you.

🕐 Create a reward system. What are some of your favorite things? (And please don't say "brown paper packages tied up with string.") Is it chocolate? Craft beers? Shoes? Relaxing with a good book? Use them as motivators. Create a reward system for yourself to do things you need to do, but don't want to do. Promise yourself that after folding and putting away all the laundry you can indulge in that high-end chocolate stashed in the back of the fridge. Reward yourself for attending that boring networking event by indulging in an evening on the couch with a good book. You get the idea. The trick with the reward system is to not give in to the reward until after the task is complete. Warning: with no one around to police you, that last part is easier said than done.

🕐 Join groups with regular meetings to create accountability. If you're having trouble remaining accountable to yourself, join a group of people trying to accomplish the same thing, so you can stay accountable to them. If you want to write a book, join a writing club that sets milestone writing goals and has meetings where members report on their progress. If you're trying to lose weight, join one of the many weight-loss groups that has regular check-ins. If you'd like to learn a new skill, consider taking a class at a local college where you're graded for your attendance and participation. Knowing your effort and progress will be seen by other people can be a huge motivator. And bonus: if you host meetings at your house, you may even be motivated to wash those dirty dishes.

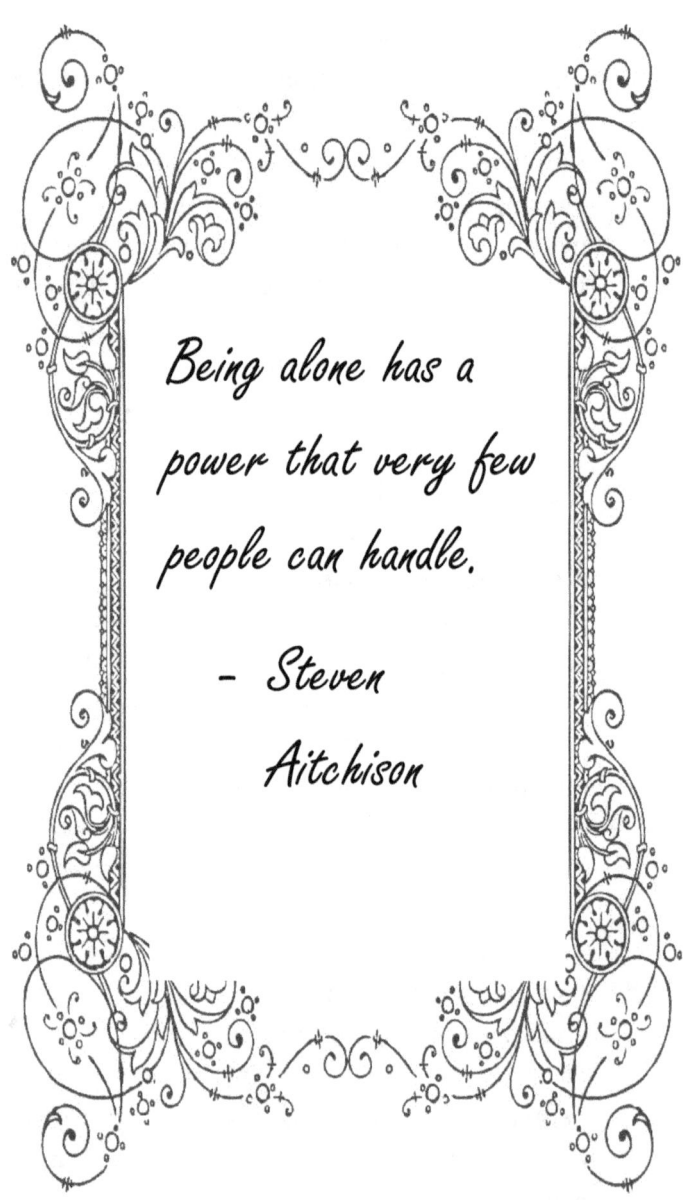

*Being alone has a power that very few people can handle.*

*— Steven Aitchison*

# 16

# ONE LAST THING

Life is hard. This is the ugly truth that most of us face when we leave the nest of home and strike out on our own. Many will choose a path of coupledom – whether with a significant other or roommate that enables them to share the burdens of life. And that's great.

But an increasing number of us have chosen another path – that of solo living – which leaves the burdens squarely on our shoulders. And that's OK, too. We are strong enough to bear it. Better to remain single, than to settle for the wrong spouse just for the sake of an easier path, and wind up lonely, unhappy, or worse.

Being alone no longer carries the stigma that it did generations ago. Now it is an admirable sign of strength. It is becoming the norm. It is slowly becoming socially acceptable to purposely choose a life of solo domesticity. But that doesn't mean it's easy, or that we feel any less pressure to couple up.

It is easy – very, very easy – to succumb to the idea of what we should be. We're bombarded with it every day. Every TV show revolves around couples, families, finding/losing relationships. Even those that, on the surface seem to be about forging your own way in life, are ultimately about relationships. So it's easy to assume that we are not complete unless we, too, are part of a relationship.

That is toxic thinking.

- ♥ Relationships are good – yes.
- ♥ Relationships are a vital part of being human – of course.
- ♥ Relationships can be supportive and help us grow – sure.
- ♥ Relationships can help us feel *less* lonely – sometimes.
- ♥ Relationships can make us feel **more** lonely – sometimes.
- ♥ Being in a relationship is a requirement for leading a happy, full, and productive life – ***absolutely not***.

We singletons are paving the way for a brave new future. It can be scary to buck the trends, to have the courage to set out on our own, to face the world alone without a familiar or familial safety net. But with a little knowledge and a whole lot of fortitude, single people are redefining what it means to be a successful adult. And even though flying solo is scary, it's also very rewarding and a heck of a lot of fun.

But aside from being rewarding and fun, our lives are a gift. We owe it to God, or the Creator, or whatever life force you believe in, to live every minute of our lives, and not wait for the perfect time, or a spouse, or whatever, to begin living fully.

Life is short. We are living on borrowed time. We never know what tomorrow has in store for us. So we must make today count. It is our responsibility to overcome fear, to push aside doubt, to silence the nay-sayers, and to make our lives our own on our own terms.

As I type this, my friends are mourning the unexpected passing of a loved one. She was only 18. She didn't expect to die so young. She thought she had a long life ahead of her – plenty of time to do things she wanted to do, to live the kind of life she wanted to live, to become the person she wanted to be. But for her, tomorrow never came.

I mention this to reinforce the point that we really don't know how much time we have on this planet. So why waste a single minute waiting to start living your life?

Go ahead. Be brave and strike out on your own. Don't wait for Mr./Mrs. Right to show up before you start living your best life. Do it now!

There's no time to waste.

# REFERENCES

Conley, M. (2012, July 17). Physical Inactivity as Damaging to Health as Smoking. Retrieved from http://abcnews.go.com/Health/physical-inactivity-harmful-smoking/story?id=16797491

LaMotte, S. (2017, August 23). Can poor sleep lead to Alzheimer's or dementia? Retrieved from https://www.cnn.com/2017/07/05/health/alzheimers-sleep-dementia-study/index.html

MacLean, J. (1983). *Secrets of a Superthief.* New York: Berkley Books.

Martin, Emmie. "90% Of Americans Don't like to Cook—and It's Costing Them Thousands Each Year." *CNBC*, 27 Sept. 2017, www.cnbc.com/2017/09/27/how-much-americans-waste-on-dining-out.html.

Masnick, G. (2015, May 20). The Rise of the Single-Person Household. *Harvard Joint Center for Housing Studies.* Retrieved from http://housingperspectives.blogspot.com/2015/05/the-rise-of-single-person-household.html

Moeller, P. (2012, March 30). How to Live Alone Without

Being Lonely. Retrieved from http://articles.chicagotribune.com/2012-03-30/news/sns-201203301004usnewsusnwr201203290329alonelt100mar30_1_relationships-single-women-social-connections

Mushtaq, R., Shoib, S., Shah, T., & Mushtaq, S. (2014, September 20). Relationship Between Loneliness, Psychiatric Disorders and Physical Health ? A Review on the Psychological Aspects of Loneliness. Retrieved from https://www.ncbi.nlm.nih.gov/pmc/articles/PMC4225959/#!po=39.2857

NPD. (2014, August 6). *Consumers Are Alone Over Half of Eating Occasions As A Result of Changing Lifestyles and More Single-Person Households* [Press release]. Retrieved from https://www.npd.com/wps/portal/npd/us/news/press-releases/consumers-are-alone-over-half-of-eating-occasions-as-a-result-of-changing-lifestyles-and-more-single-person-households-reports-npd/

Oaklander, M. (2017, April 6). Science Says Your Pet Is Good for Your Mental Health. Retrieved from http://time.com/4728315/science-says-pet-good-for-mental-health/

Palmer, K. (2012, October 17). Why Single People Are So Financially Stressed. Retrieved from https://money.usnews.com/money/personal-finance/articles/2012/10/17/why-single-people-are-so-financially-stressed

Pets and mental health. (n.d.). Retrieved from https://www.mentalhealth.org.uk/a-to-z/p/pets-

and-mental-health

Pochepan, J. (2017, March 23). Bad Mood in the Workplace? Try Changing the Lights. Retrieved from https://www.inc.com/jeff-pochepan/these-office-lighting-changes-will-improve-your-mood-and-productivity.html

Ryback, R. (2016, July 11). The Powerful Psychology Behind Cleanliness. Retrieved from https://www.psychologytoday.com/us/blog/the-truisms-wellness/201607/the-powerful-psychology-behind-cleanliness

Severson, A. (2017, February 10). People are obsessed with essential oils. Here's why. Retrieved from https://www.usatoday.com/story/news/nation-now/2017/02/10/essential-oils-aromatherapy/97739568/

Taylor-Gadsby, K. (2017, October 16). Volunteering: A Formula For Help And Happiness. Retrieved from https://www.forbes.com/sites/forbescoachescouncil/2017/10/16/volunteering-a-formula-for-help-and-happiness/#591fdb63cdc3

U.S. Census Bureau. (2016, August 26). FFF: Unmarried and Single Americans Week: Sept. 18-24, 2016. Retrieved from https://www.census.gov/newsroom/facts-for-features/2016/cb16-ff18.html

Zagorsky, J. (2016, June 3). Why are fewer people getting married? Retrieved from https://news.osu.edu/news/2016/06/03/why-are-fewer-people-getting-married/

# ABOUT THE AUTHOR

Jennifer Lynn O'Hara is a busy actress, singer, musician, artist, photographer, and author. She has appeared in numerous television and film projects and a multitude of stage productions, is a published poet and author, and has had her art shown in several exhibits. She is the author of *Four Extra Hours*, the regular host of the series, *A Single Girl's Guide To…*, as well as an avid DIY-er and recipe creator.

Jennifer lives by the beach in Southern California with her two cats.

Follow Jennifer on Instagram at @jenniferlynnohara, and via the travel, cooking, and lifestyle website asinglegirlsguideto.com.

# FOUR EXTRA HOURS

by Jennifer Lynn O'Hara

How many times have you said, "If I only had the time I'd..."? Or, "If I just had more time in the day I'd..."? With a few easy-to-incorporate changes to your daily habits, you can feasibly liberate four hours each week from your hectic schedule. With those extra hours, you can start to cross things off your "someday" list.

This book shows you how to find four extra hours in your week, and offers over 200 ideas of life-enriching ways to spend that new-found time.

Available now on Amazon.com.

www.ingramcontent.com/pod-product-compliance
Lightning Source LLC
Chambersburg PA
CBHW051650040426
42446CB00009B/1062